ALPHABET

A B C D E
F G H I J K
L M N O P
Q R S T U
V W X Y Z

CLARELLEN
©2013 Douglas Holleley
Rochester, NY
ISBN 978-0-9895939-0-8

A B C D E
F G H I J K
L M N O P
Q R S T U
V W X Y Z

DOUGLAS HOLLELEY

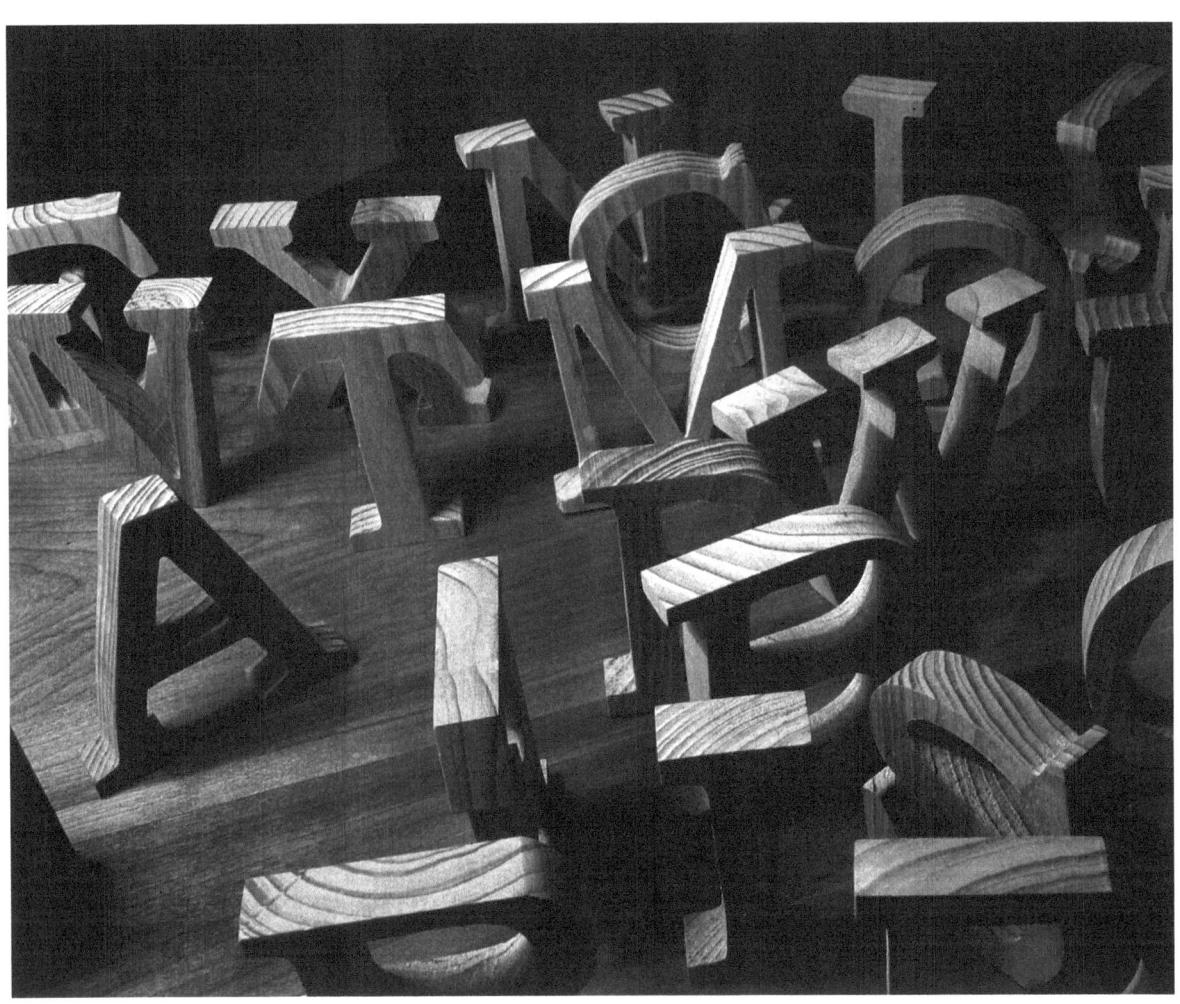

October 20, 2011.
Individual letters photographed on the kitchen table in Rochester.

ALPHABET

THE ALPHABET PROJECT—NATURE OF THE STUDY

Initial Hypothesis: To investigate the behavior of snow as it accumulates on a low-relief, three-dimensional object—in this case an alphabet of wooden letters.

Subsequent Hypothesis: Once the season changed it seemed appropriate to see how other "things that fall from the sky" might interact with the alphabet.

METHOD

Purchase letters from art supply store, stain them with India ink, attach them to a suitable substrate and begin to photograph.

TIME AND PLACE

The project commenced in November 2011 with the construction of the mounted alphabet. The actual photographing started around Christmas 2011 and continued for a year. Unless noted otherwise, all the images were made in the yard of my home in Rochester, NY.

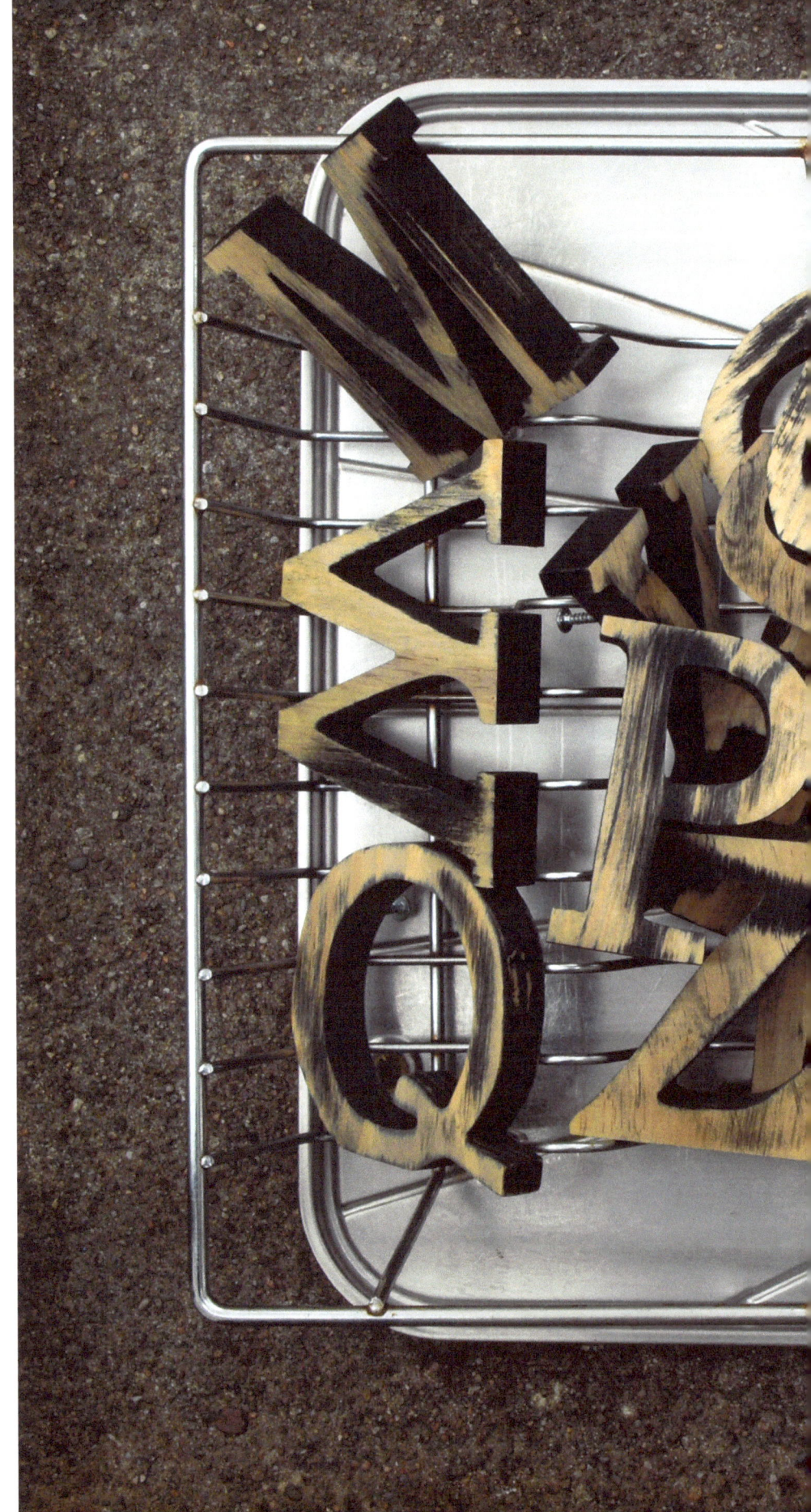

November 3, 2011.

After an initial sanding, the letters were stained with India ink, sanded again, and then washed prior to a second application of ink.

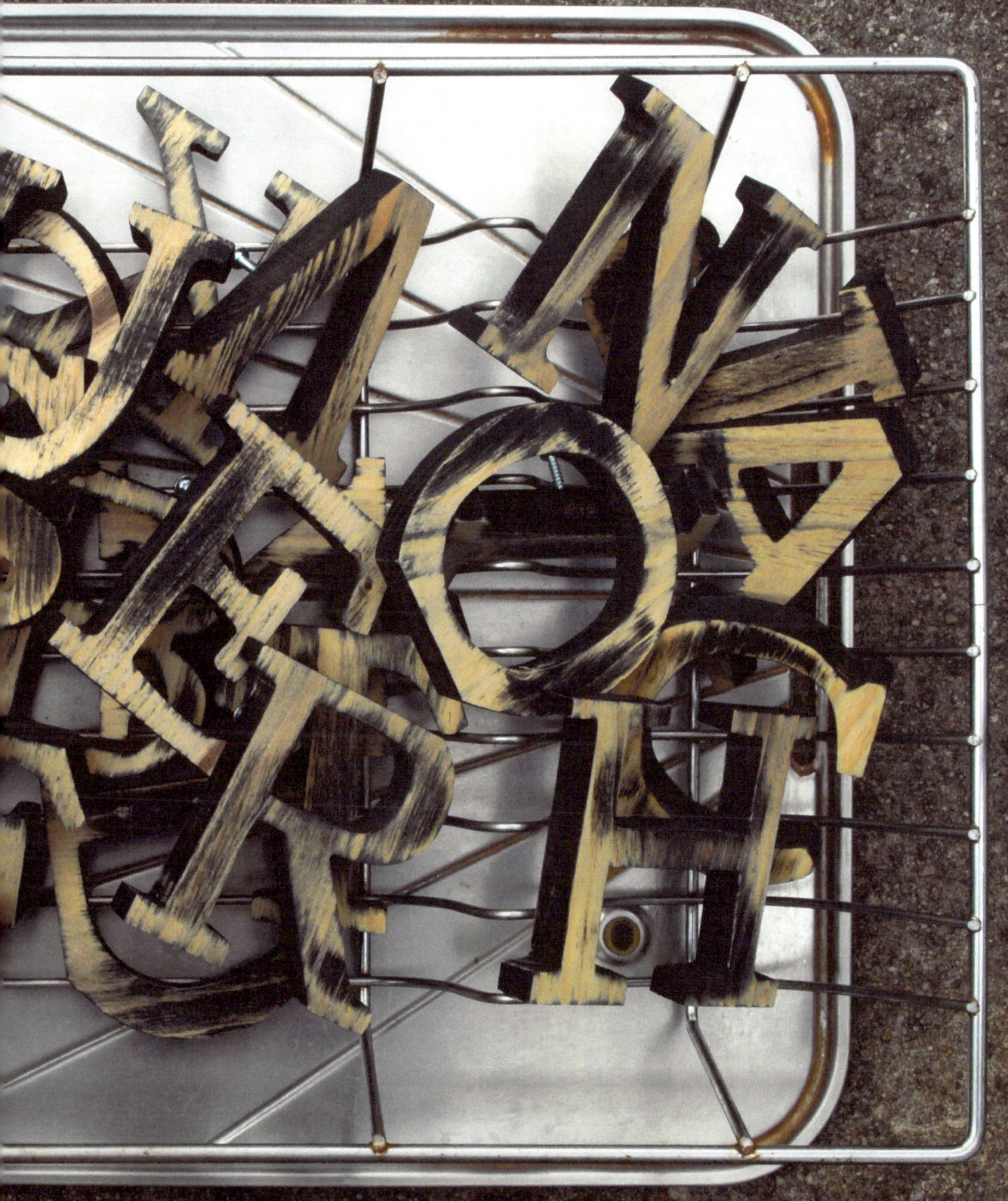

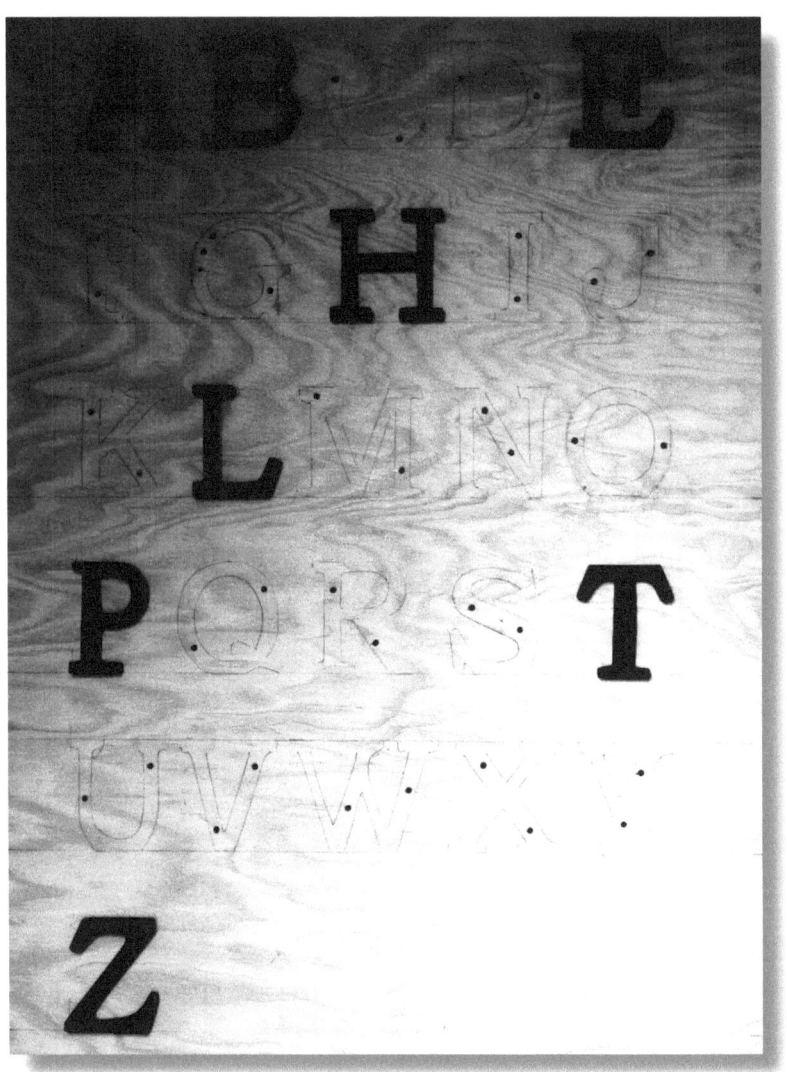

December 3, 2011.
Laying out the letters on a plywood base before attaching them with screws.

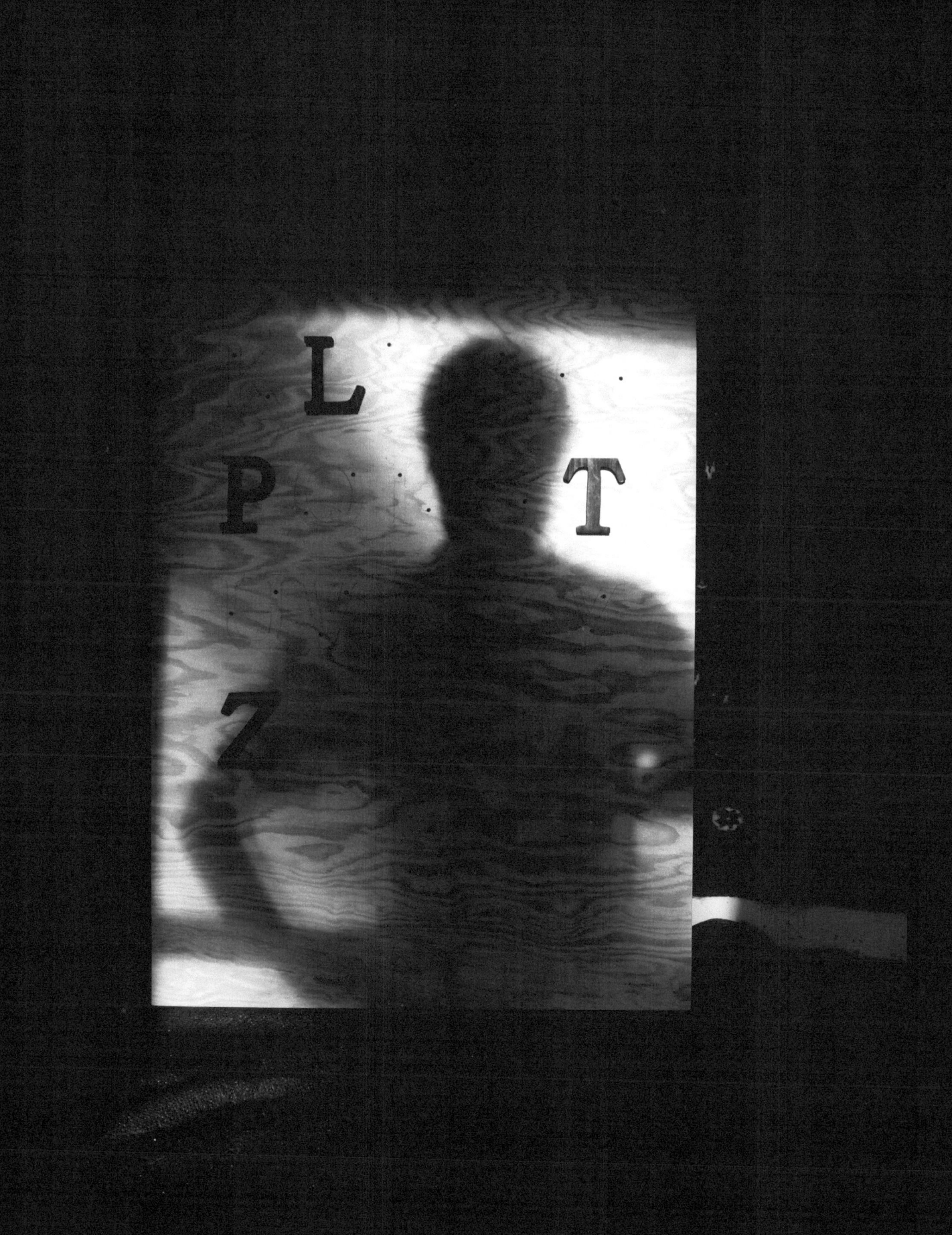

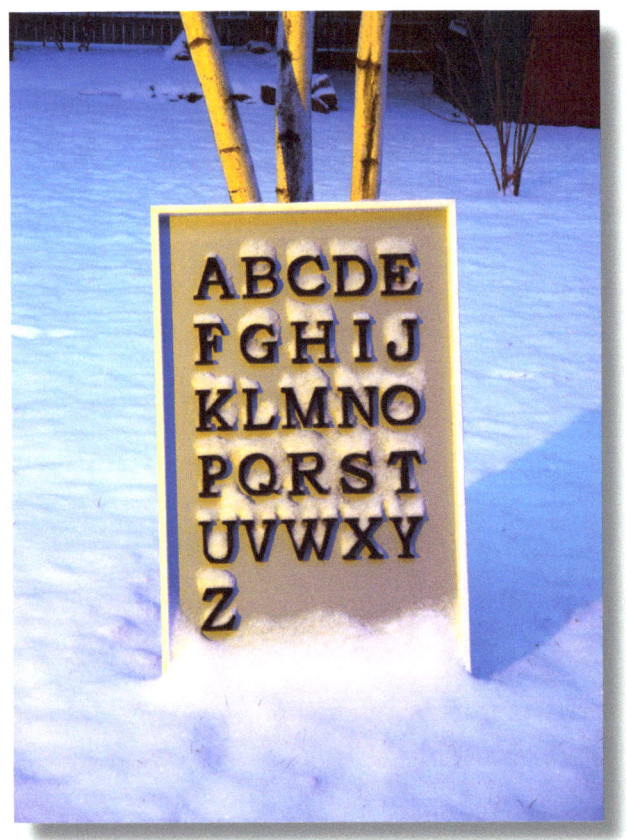

December 28, 2011.

As I have said on another occasion, "Thank Heavens for perversity. Otherwise we couldn't count on anything." I say this because after making a device specifically designed to catch snow, as it turned out the winter of 2011–12 was one of the warmest on record. As such, there was snow yes, but nothing like the 120 inches that is normal for Rochester, NY.

The image above was made in the evening after the grid on the opposite page had been photographed during the day.

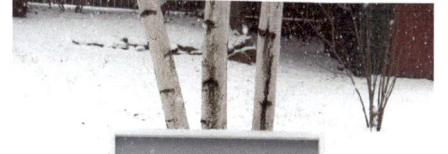
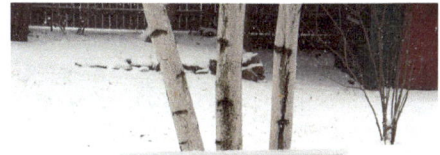
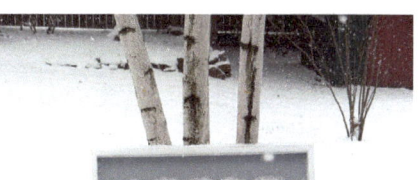
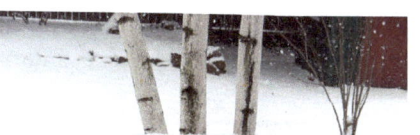
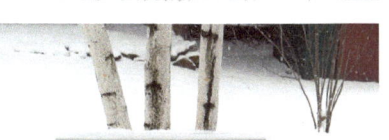
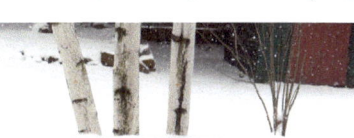
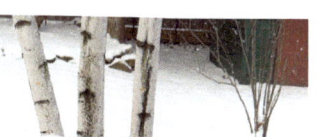
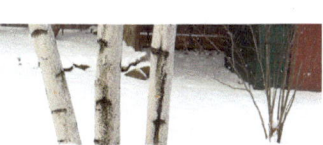
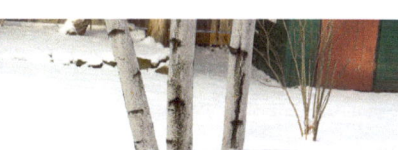

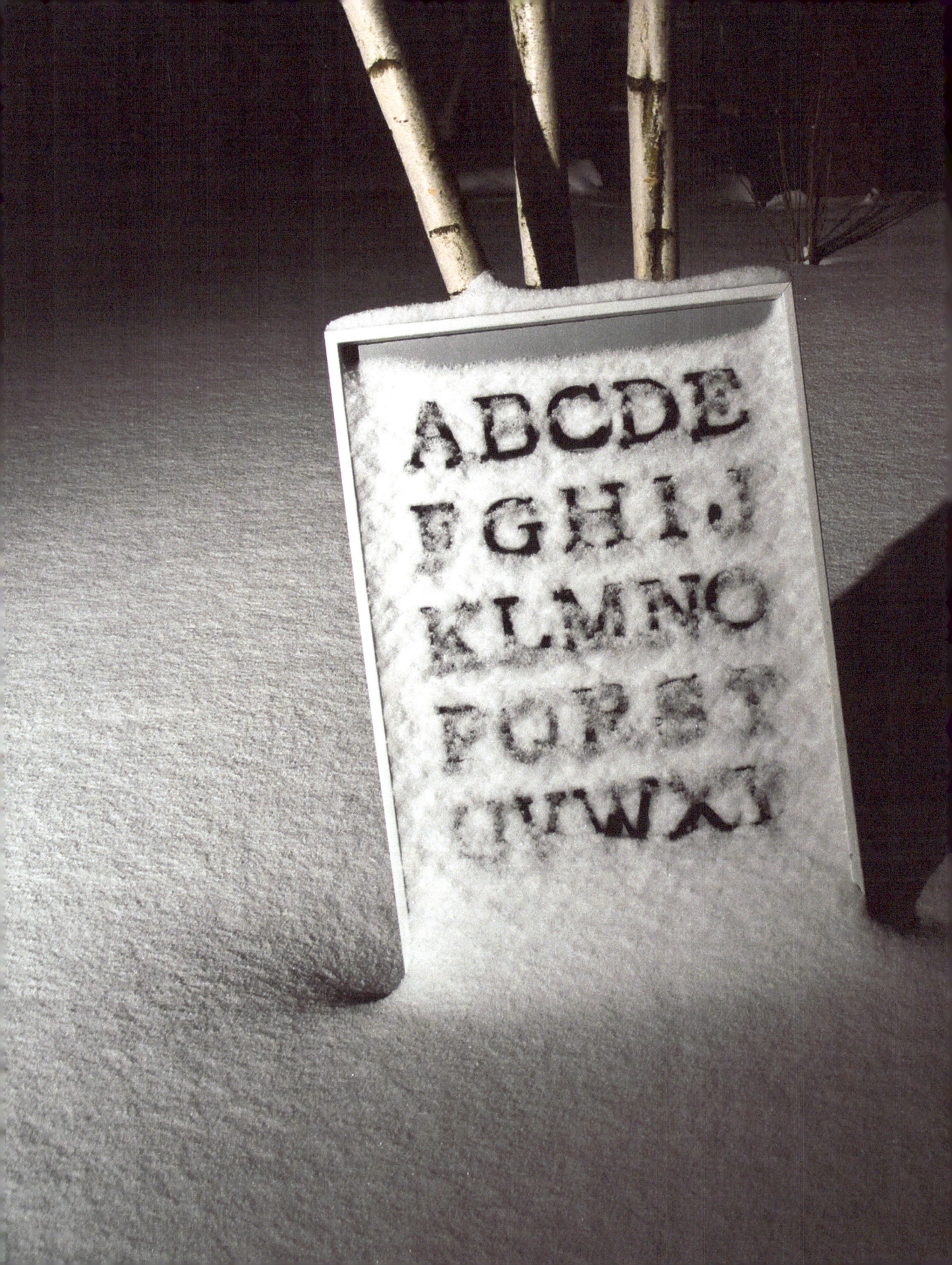

January 13, 2012.

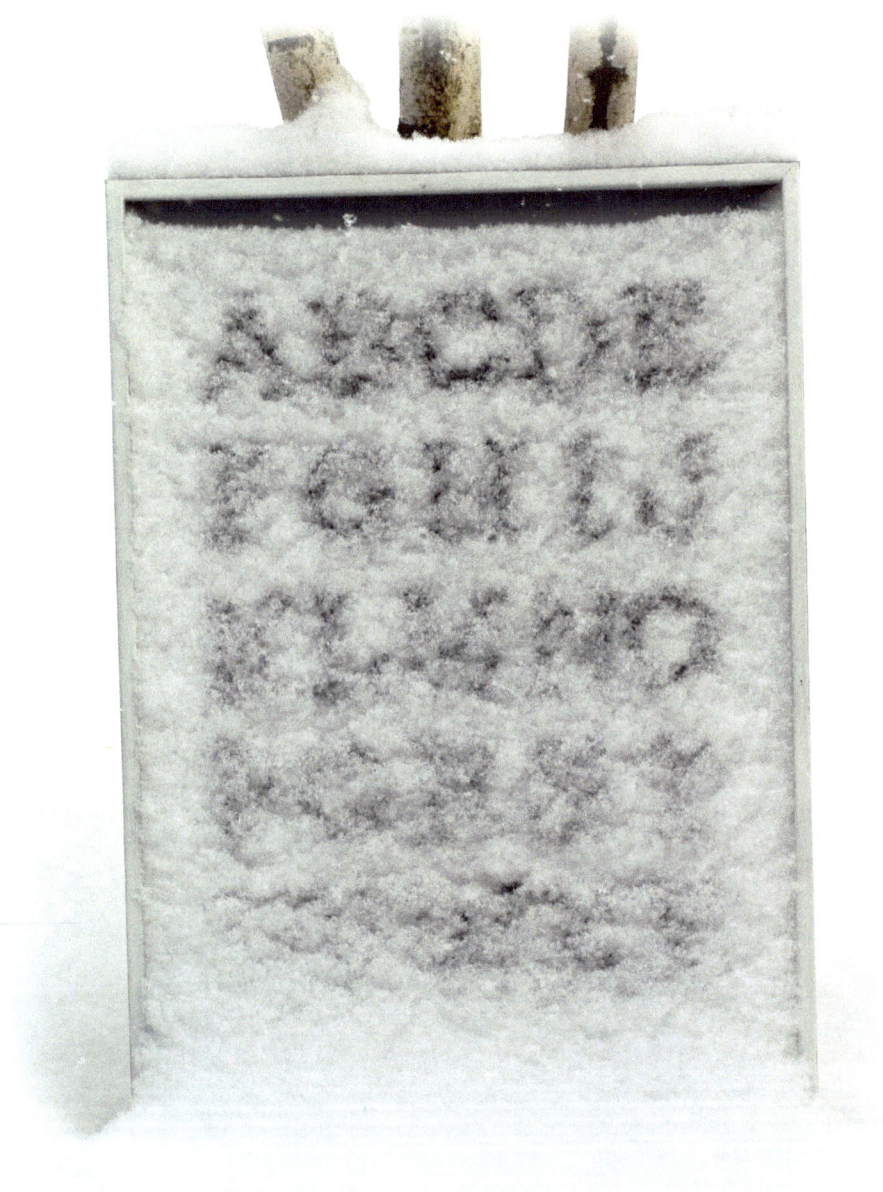

January 13–14, 2012.

The image above was made during the day of January 13, prior to the night image on the preceding spread. The sequential grid on the opposite page was photographed on the 14th.

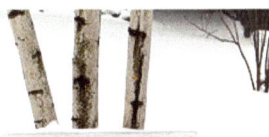
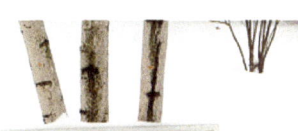

January 15, 2012.

ABCDE
FGHIJ
KLMNO
PQRST
UVWXY

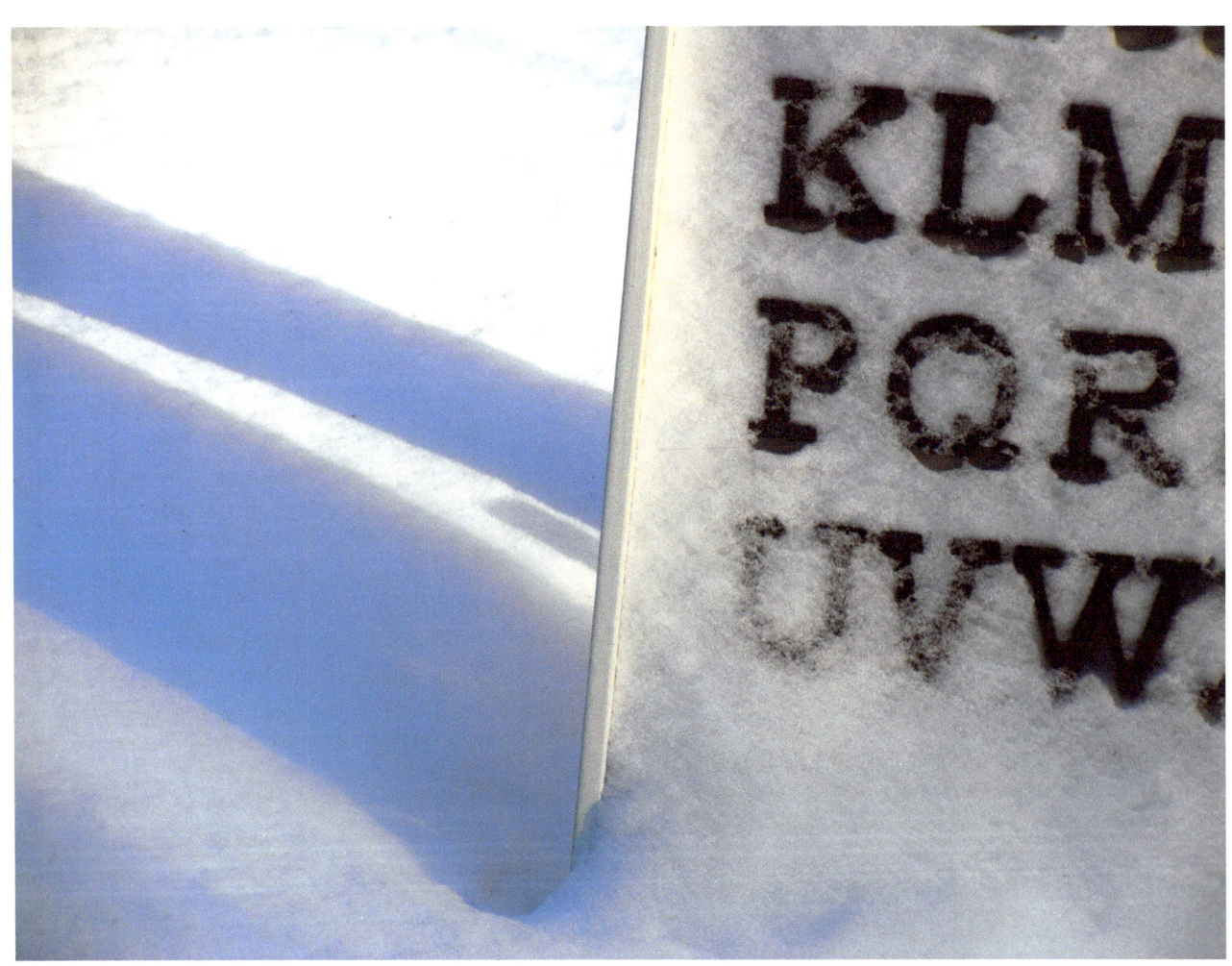

January 15, 2012.
Image above and opposite made on this day.

ABCDE
FGHIJ
KLMNO
PQRST
UVWXY

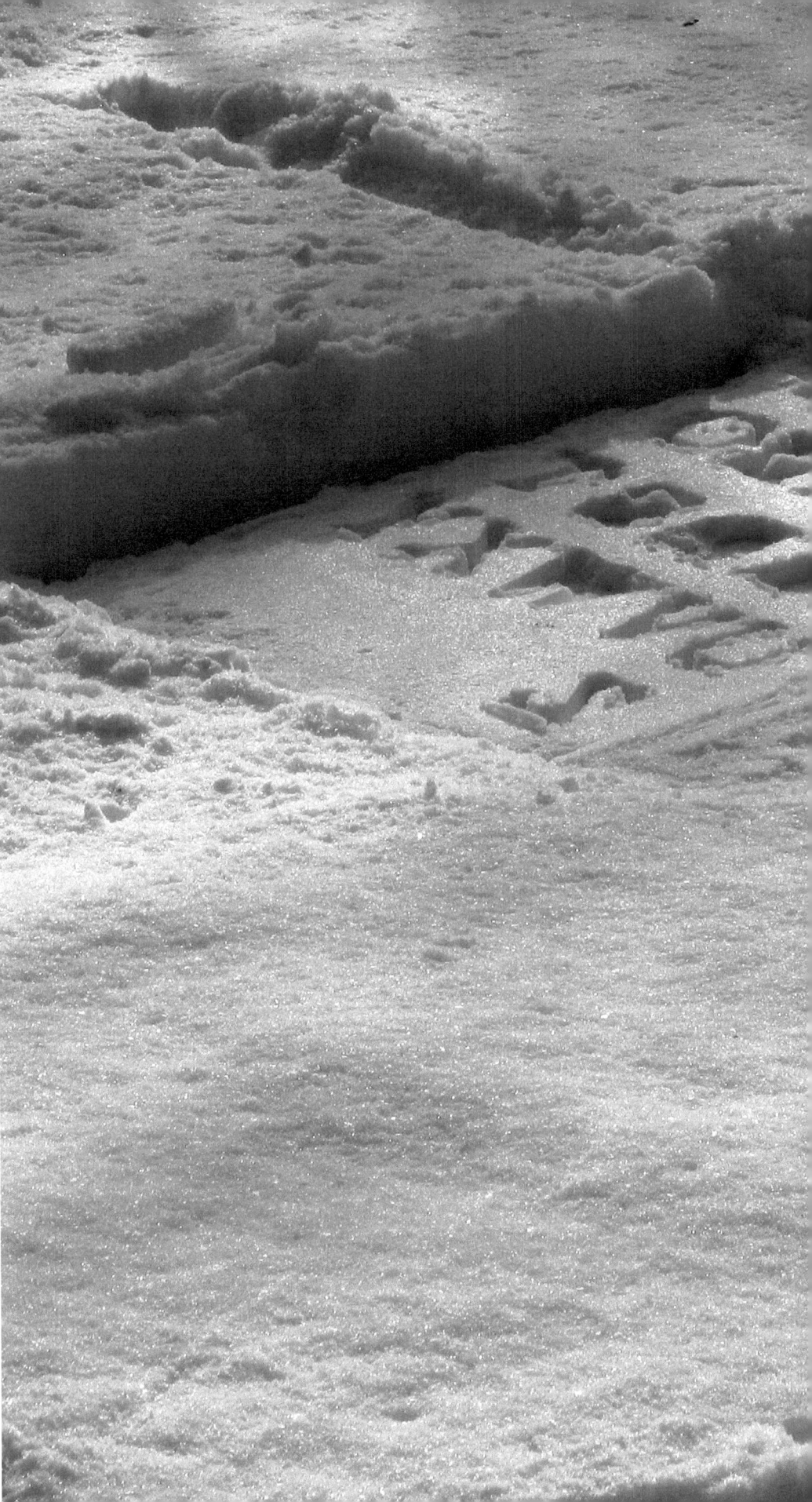

January 16, 2012.

Instead of permitting the snow to fall on the letters, here the alphabet has been used as a matrix to imprint the letter-forms into the fallen snow.

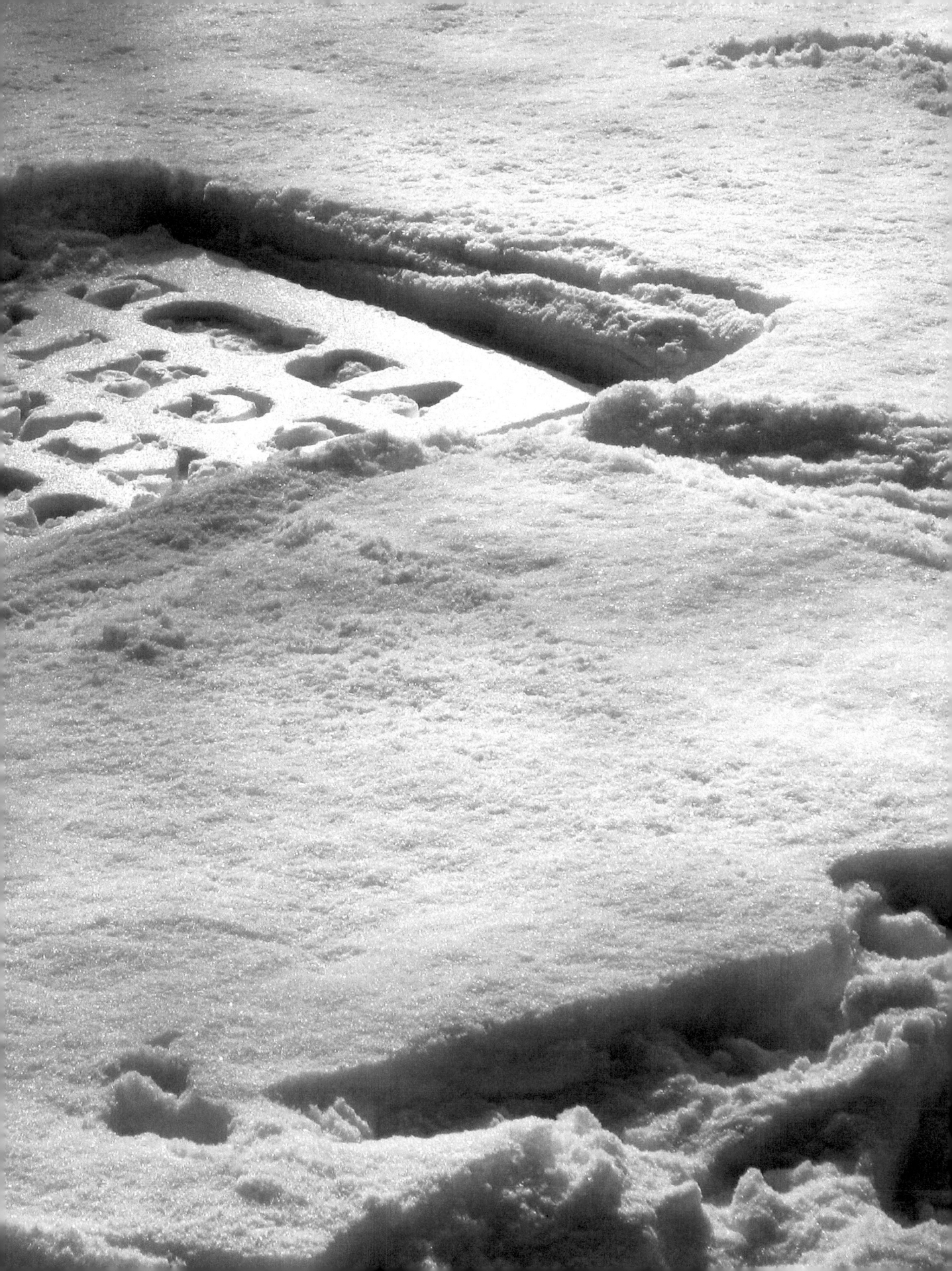

January 19, 2012.

ABCDE
FGHIJ
KLMNO
PQRST
UVWXY
Z

January 29, 2012.

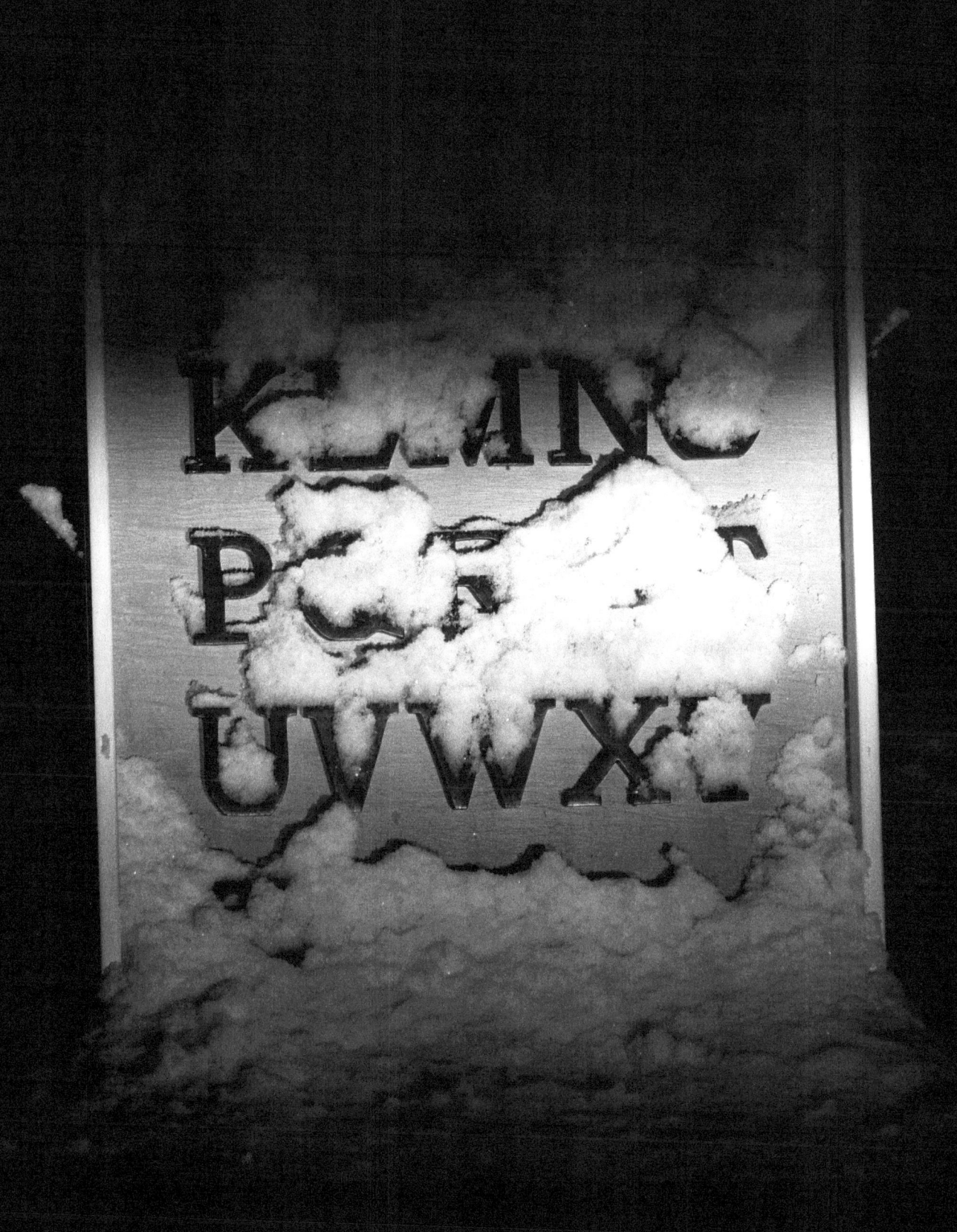

January 30, 2012.

K L M N O

J V W X

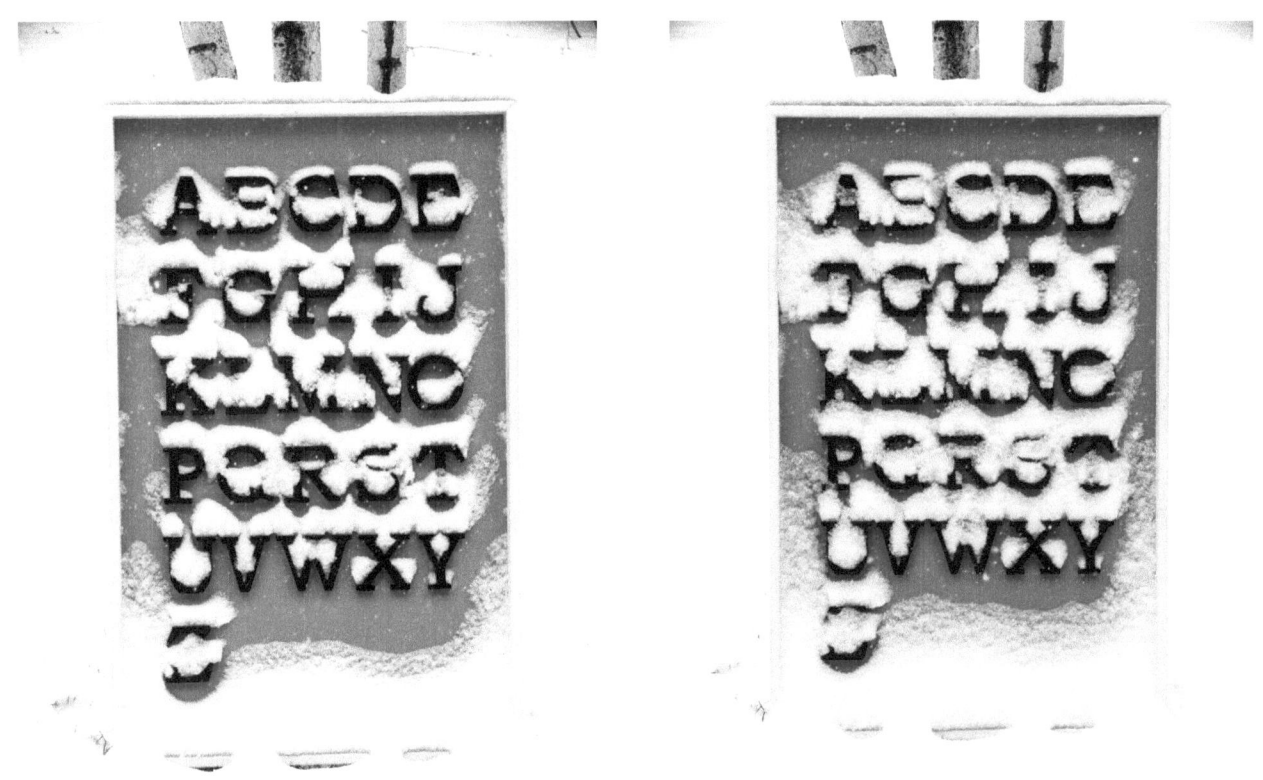

February 11, 2012.

A B C D E
F G H I J
K L M N O
P Q R S T
U V W X Y

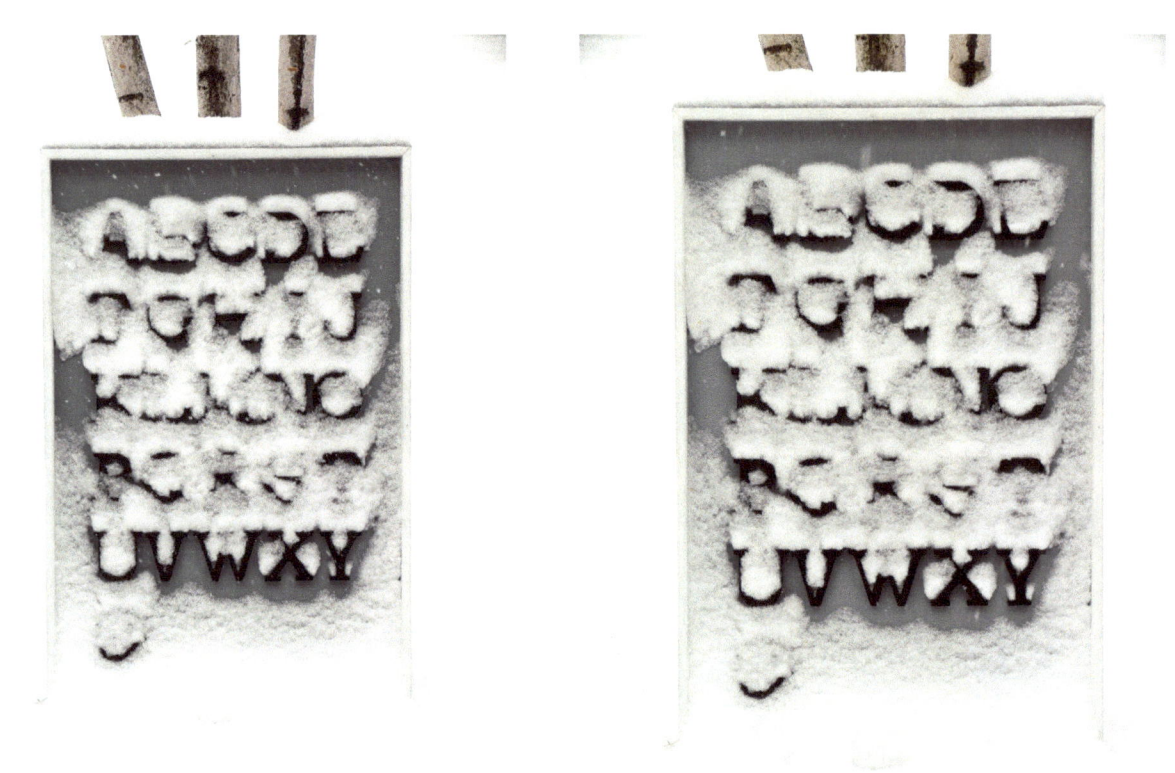

February 11, 2012.

February 12, 2012.

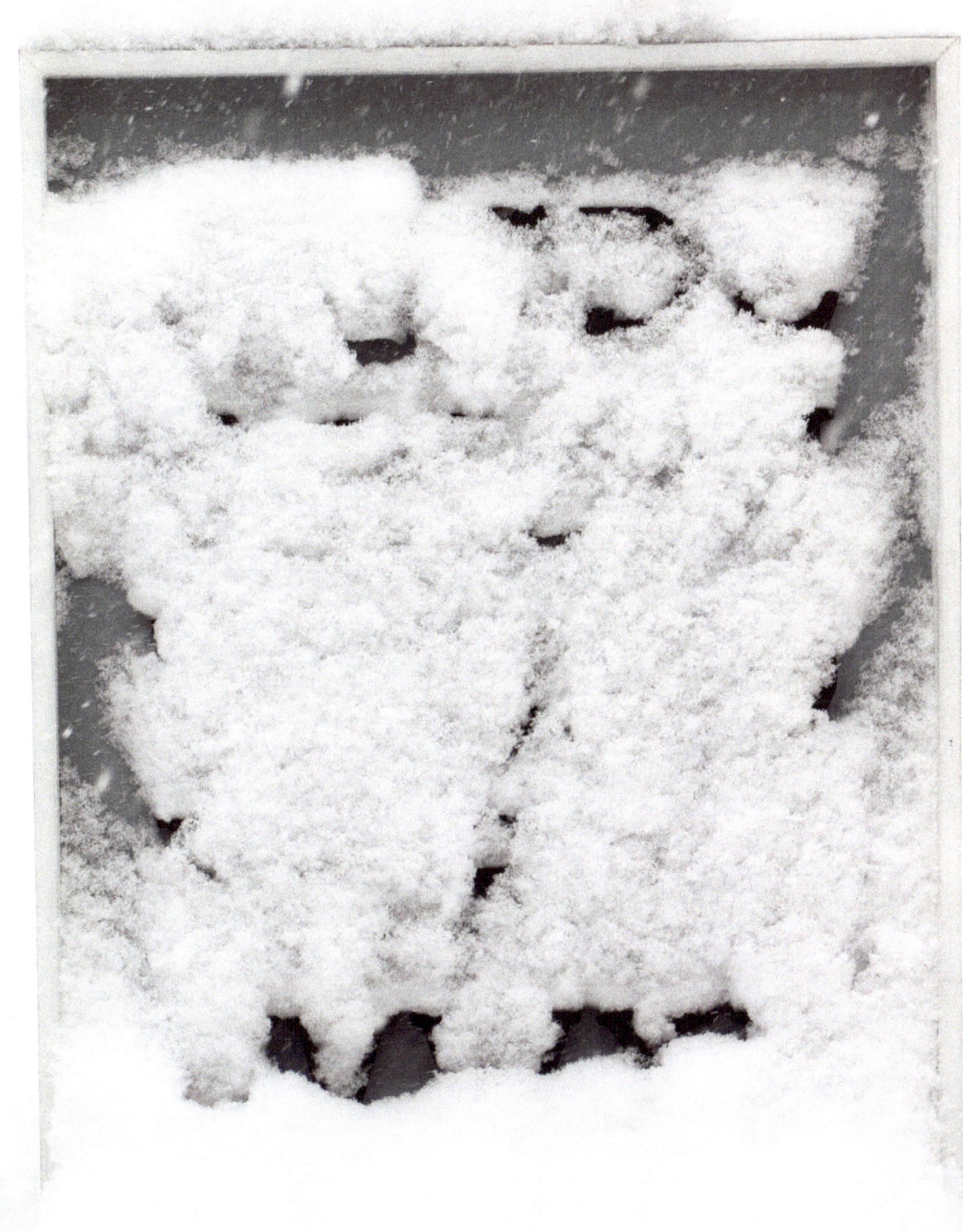

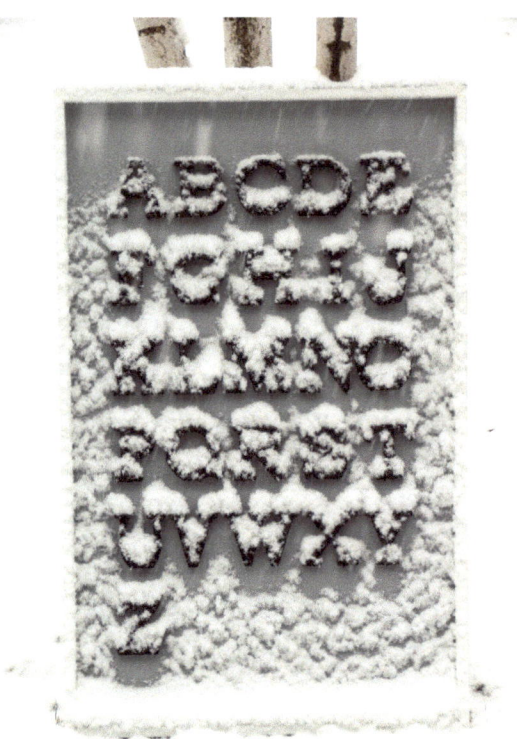

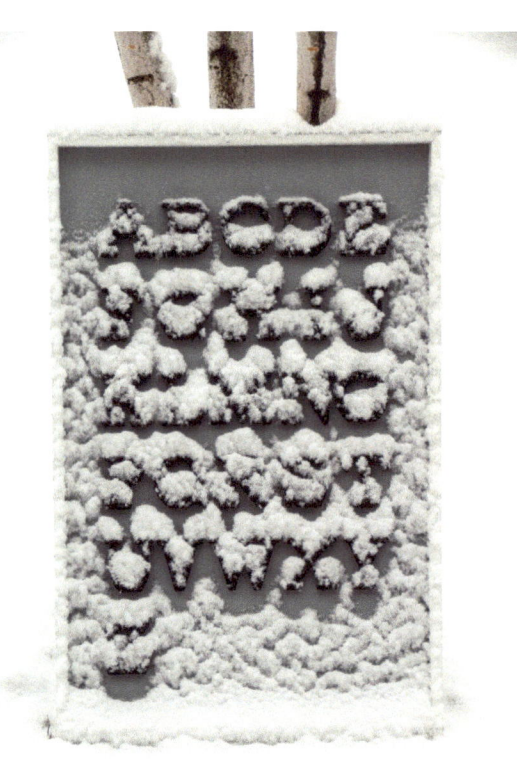

February 18, 2012.

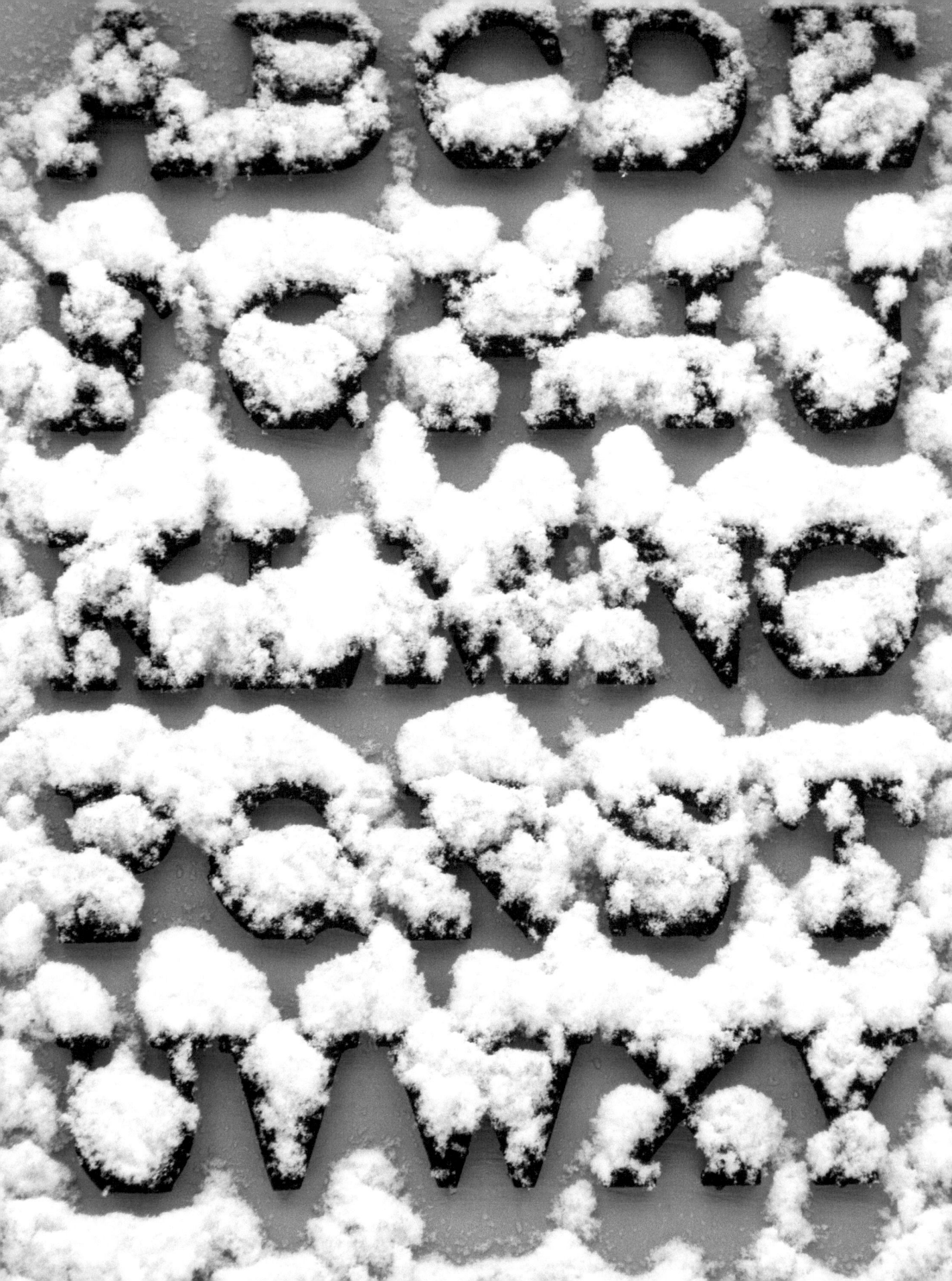

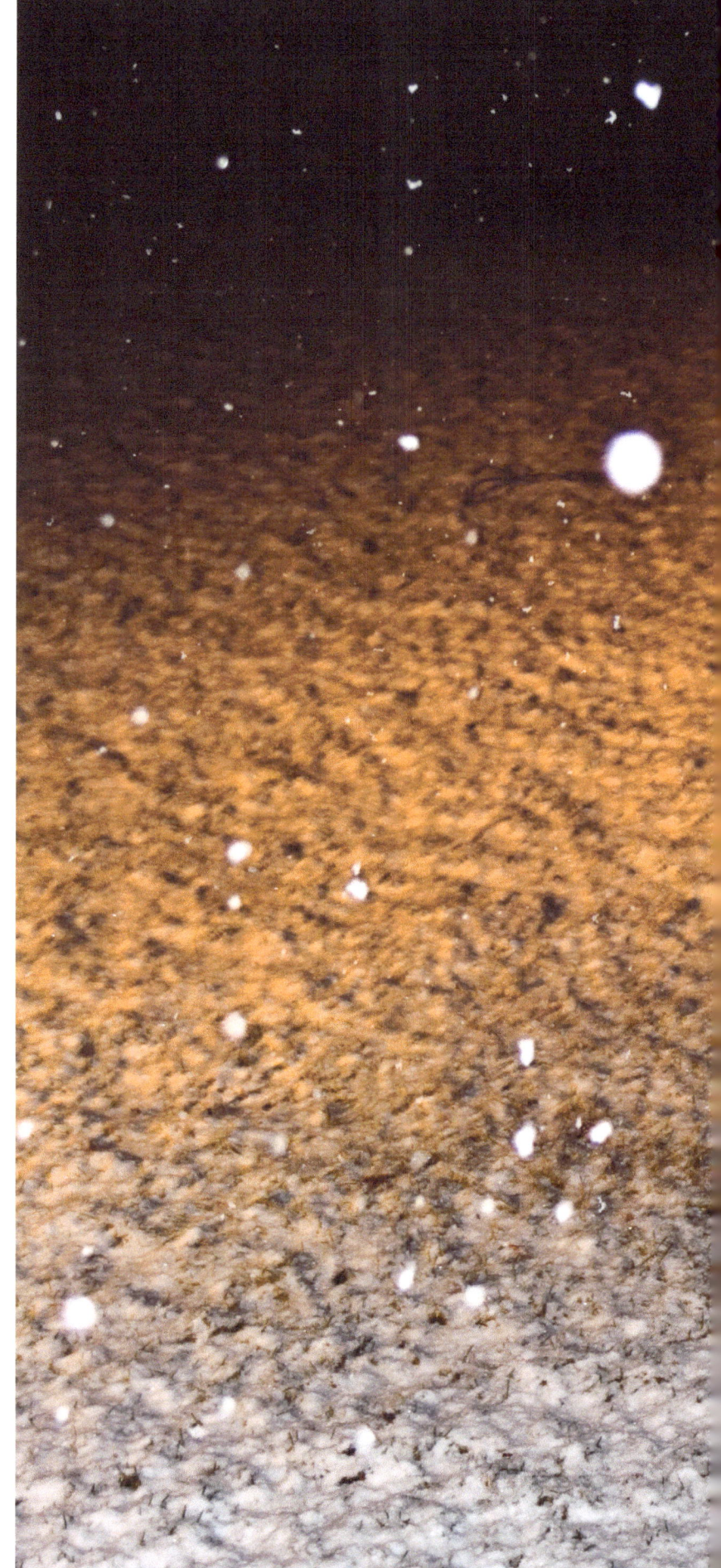

February 21, 2012.

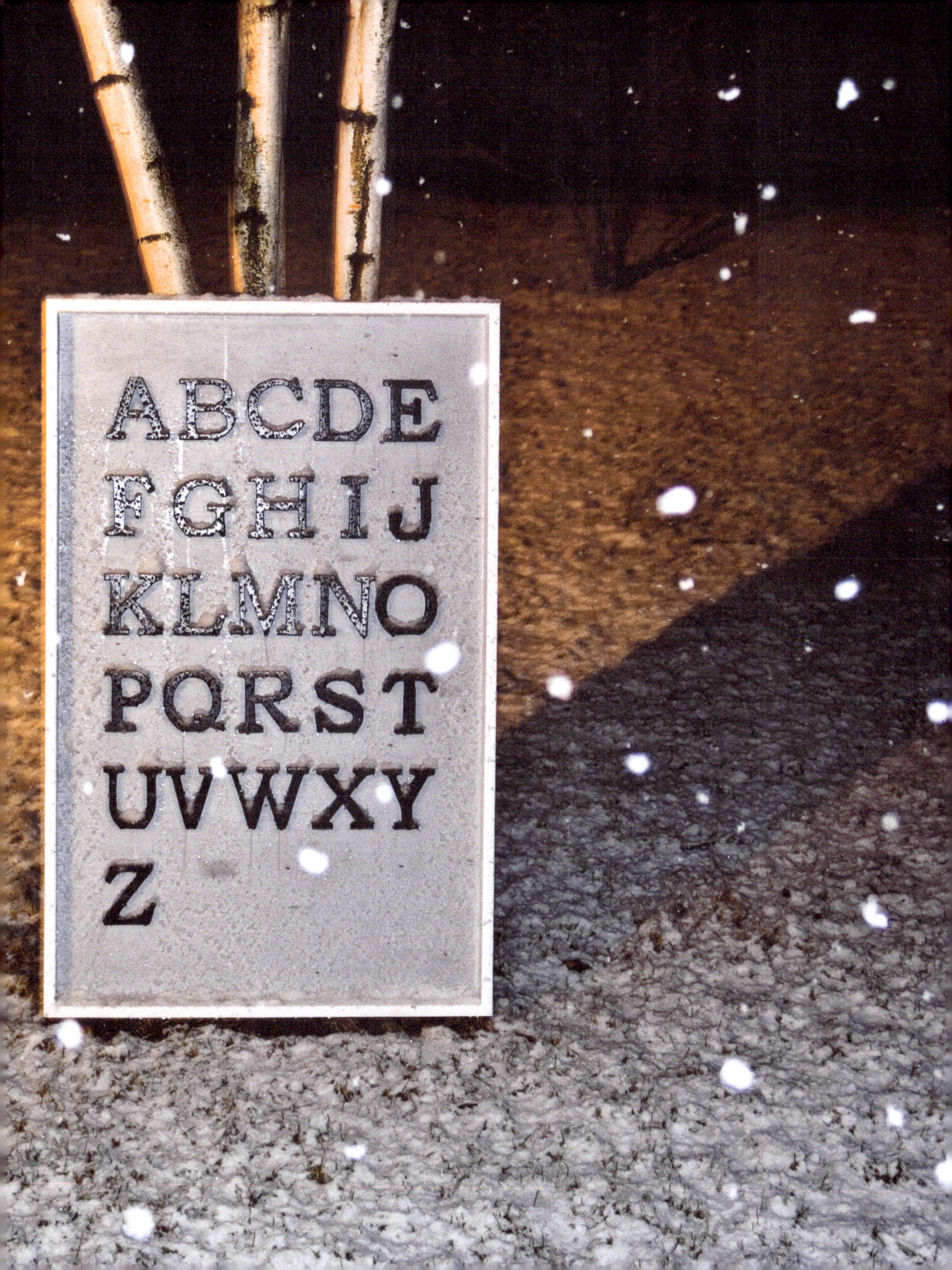
ABCDE
FGHIJ
KLMNO
PQRST
UVWXY
Z

February 25, 2012.

ABCDE
FGHIJ
KLMNO
PQRST
UVWXY

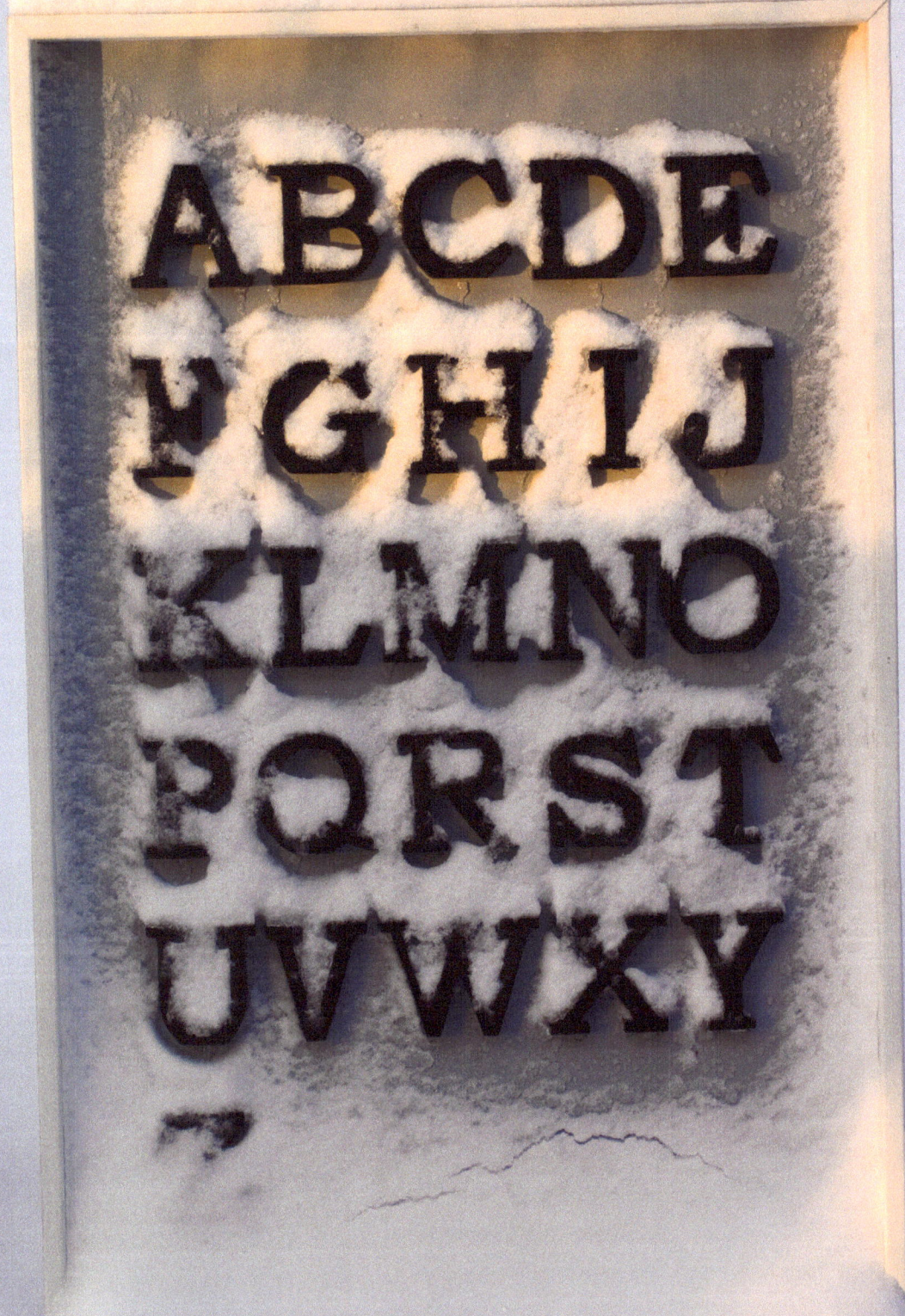

February 25, 2012.

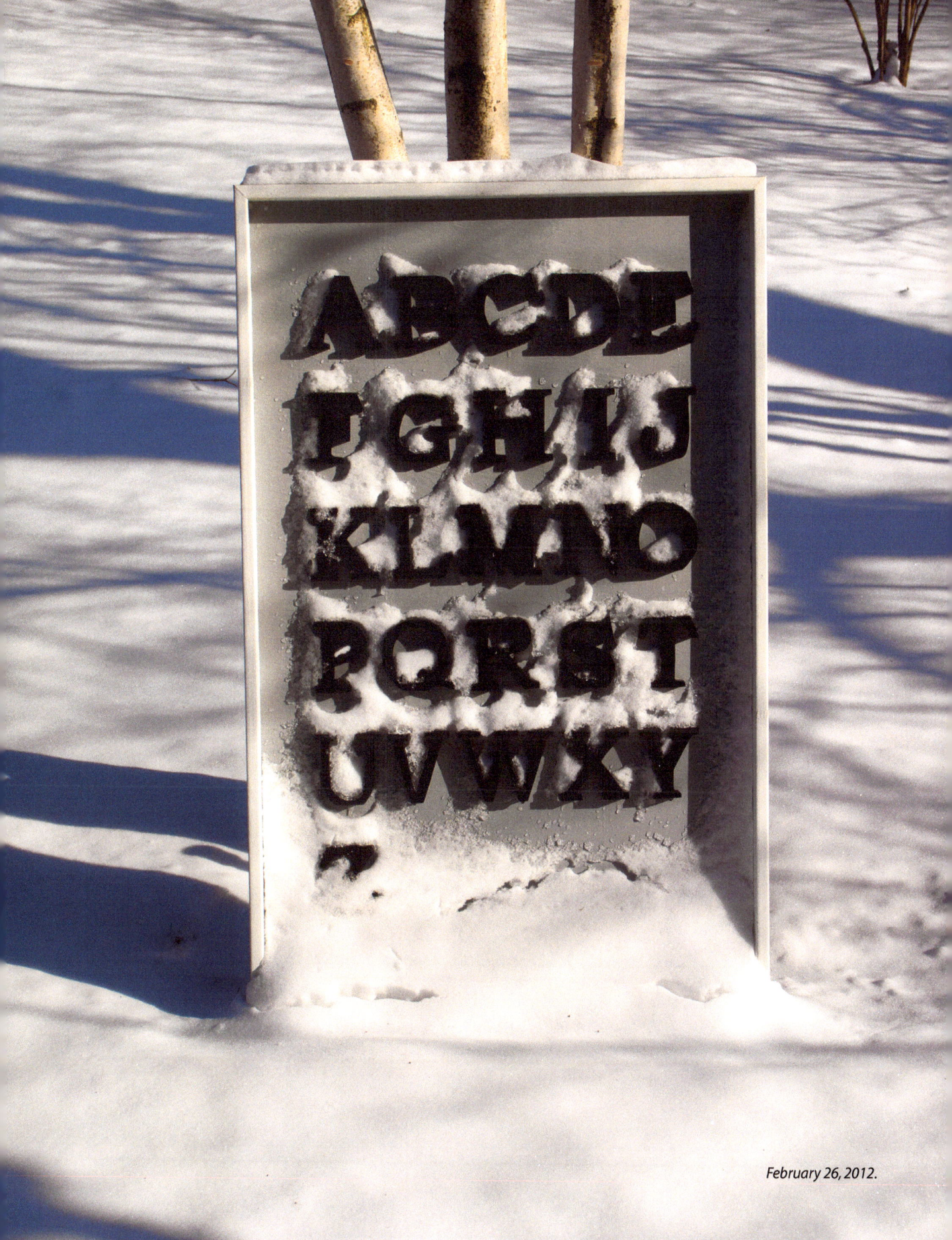

February 26, 2012.

March 3, 2012.

By this date, the unusually warm winter was beginning to come to an end. As the image opposite shows, it was warm enough for me to wash the letters. I realized that the winter component of the project was about to finish whether I liked it or not.

Seeing the letters under the surface of the water gave me an idea. Hoping the cold weather would last a little longer, even if only overnight, I laid the alphabet on its back, and on the evening of March 5, I filled it with water and hoped the temperature would drop below freezing. Fortunately, it did.

The image on the following spread was made on the morning of March 6 when I was able to persuade the ice to come away from the letters and lie on my black background cloth on the driveway. Sadly it soon broke ito several large chunks but I was able to get a number of images before it melted away.

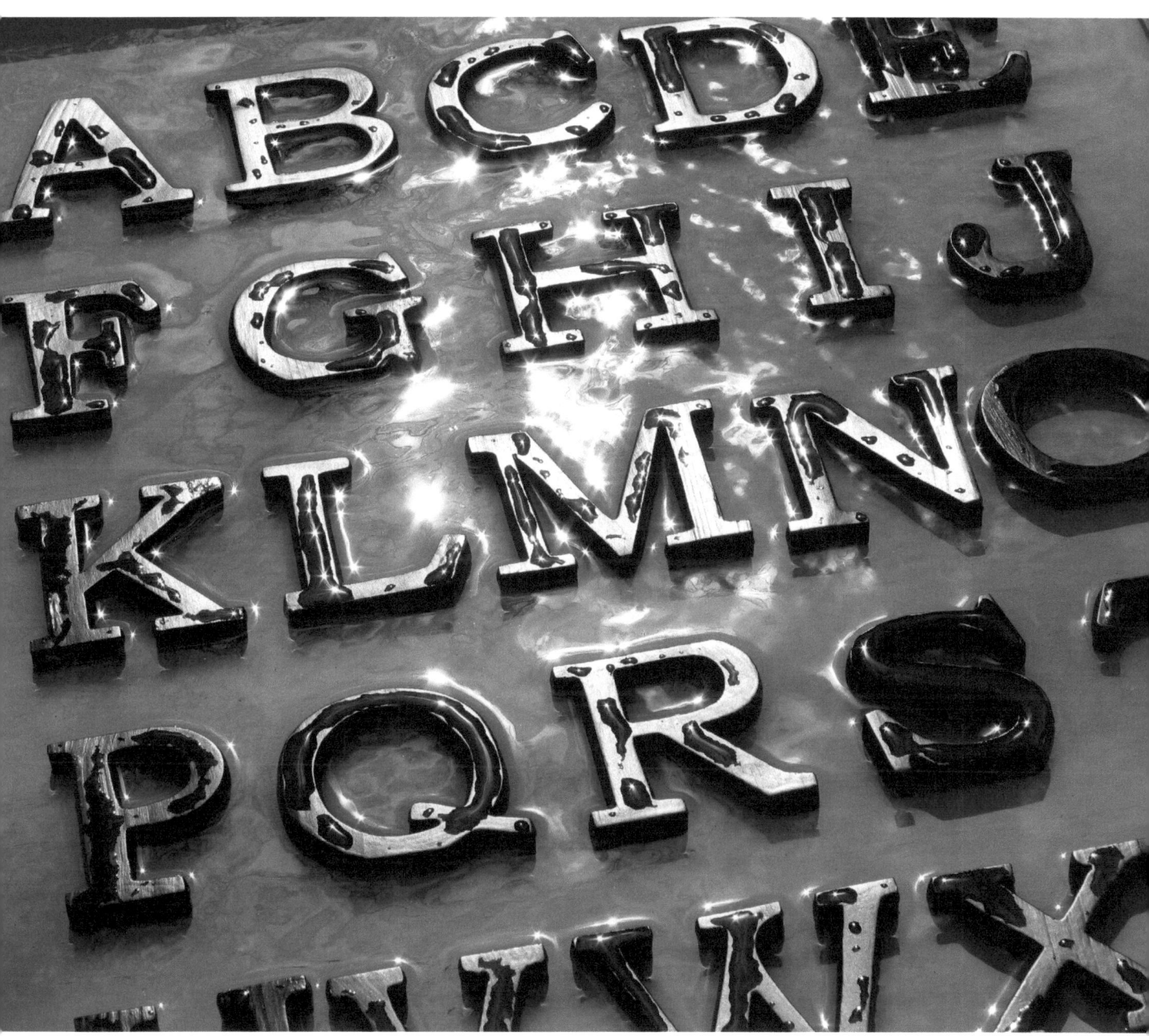

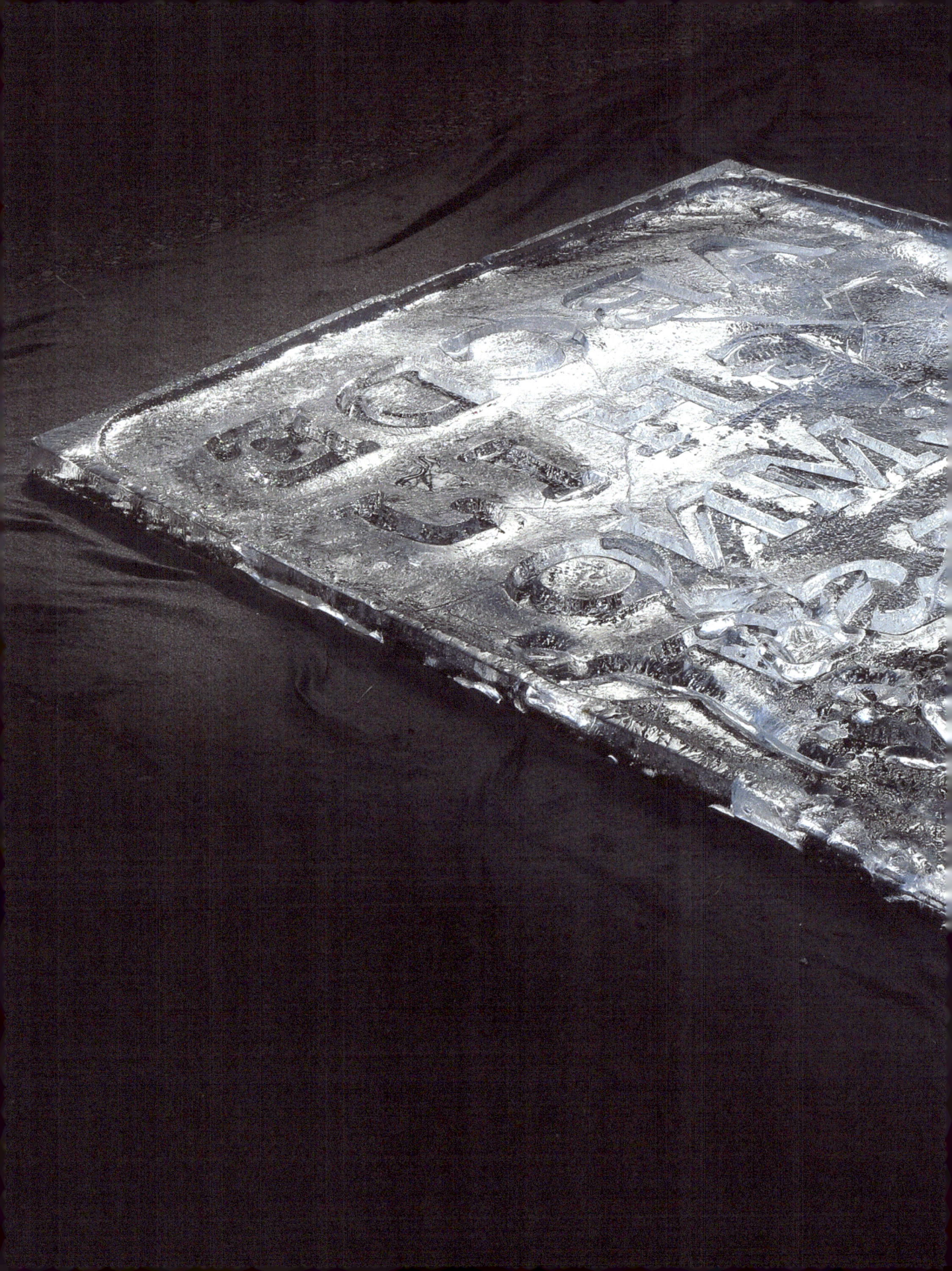

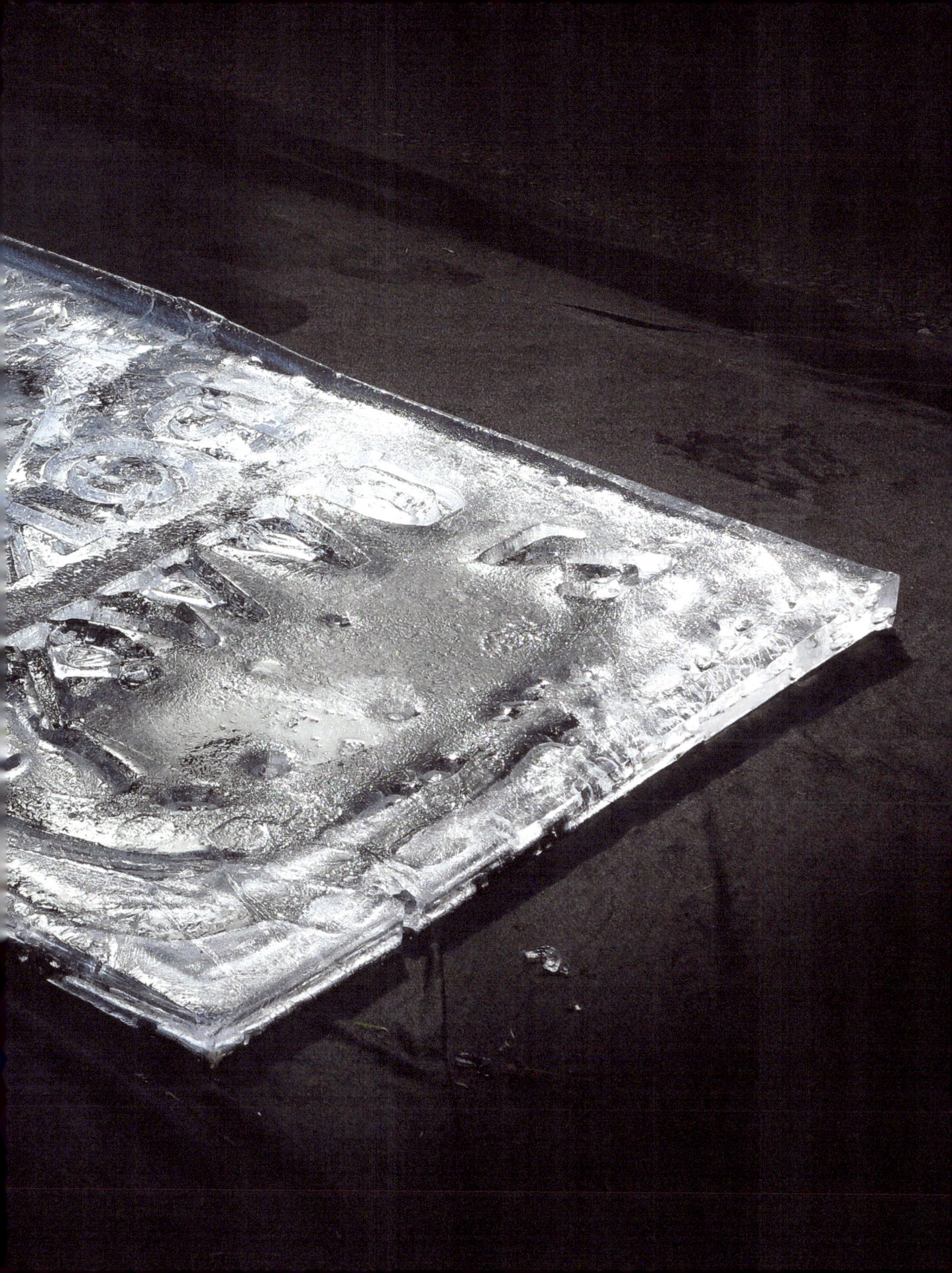

March 6, 2012.

Detail of the frozen alphabet shown on the preceding spread. You will observe that the letters are reversed. I attempted to turn the cast ice over to view the letters in their normal orientation but as I did the cast broke. The two following pages show a couple of the larger fragments.

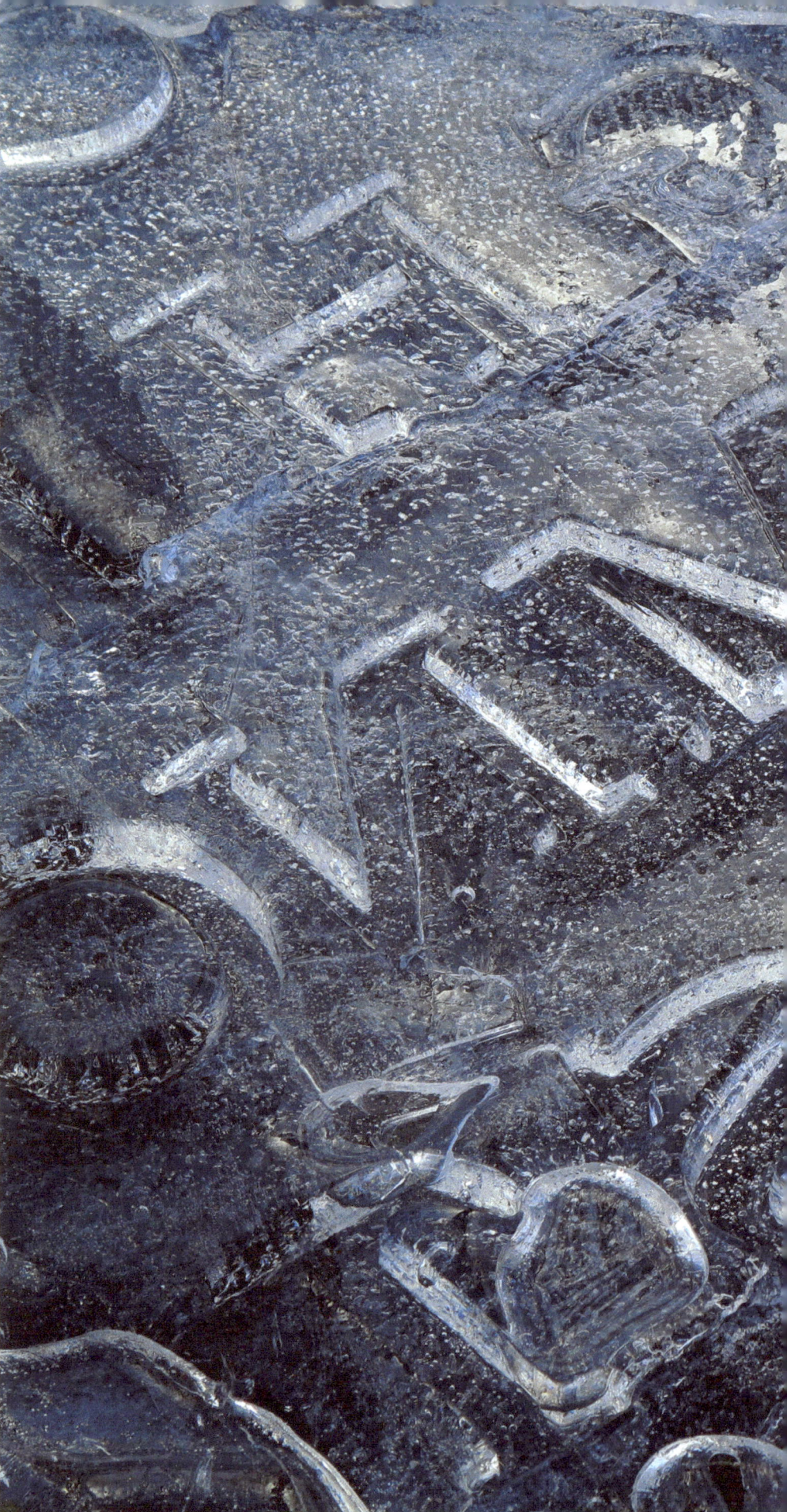

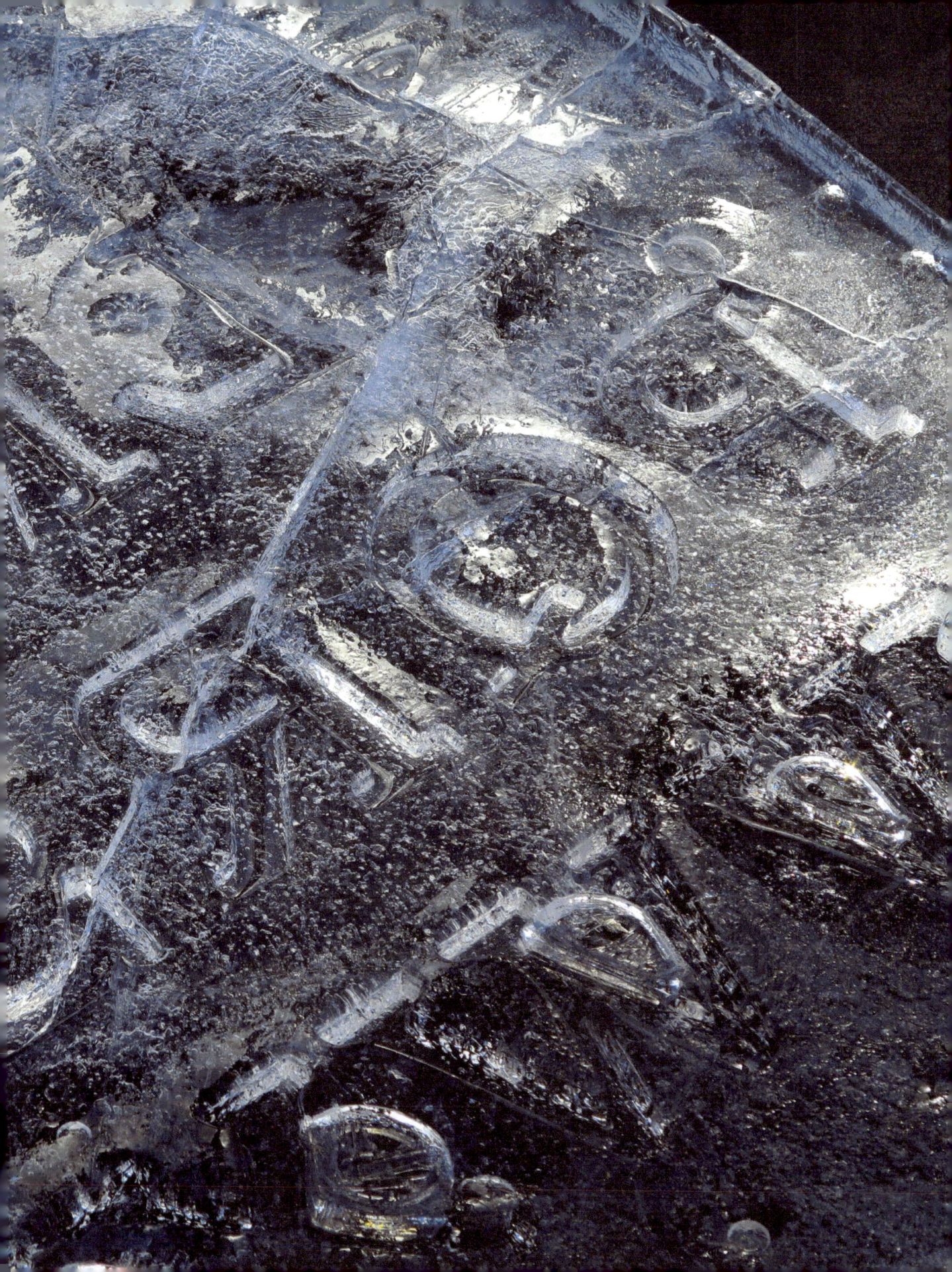

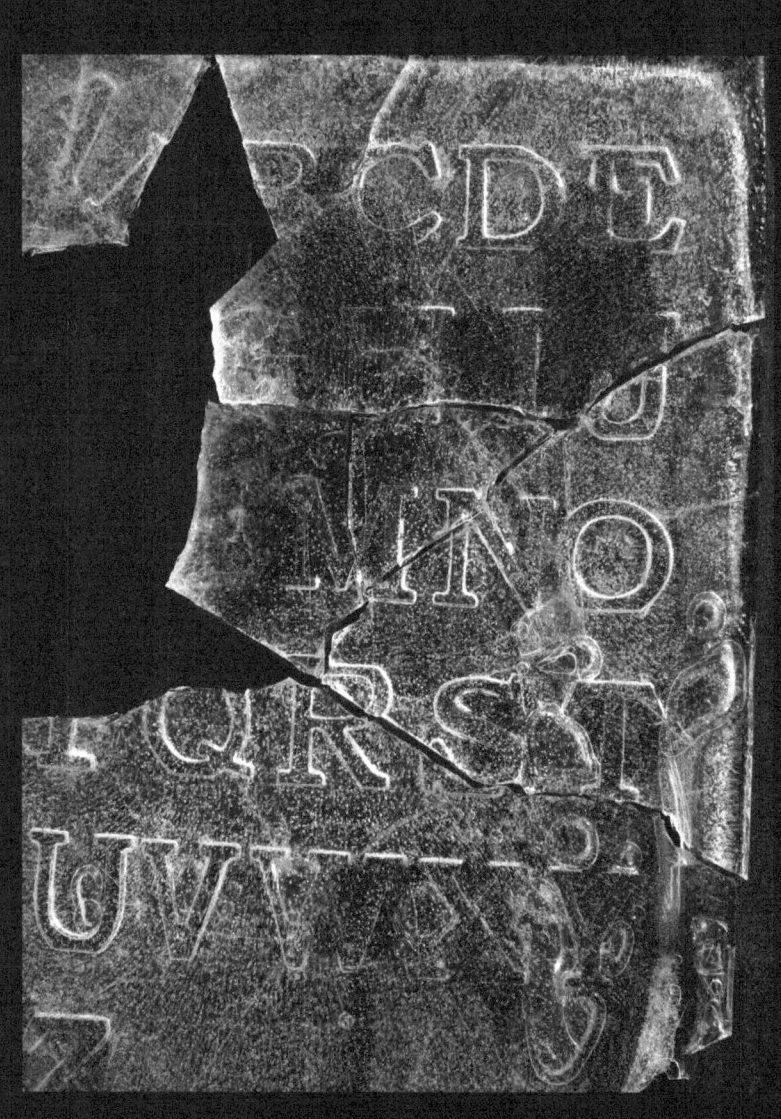

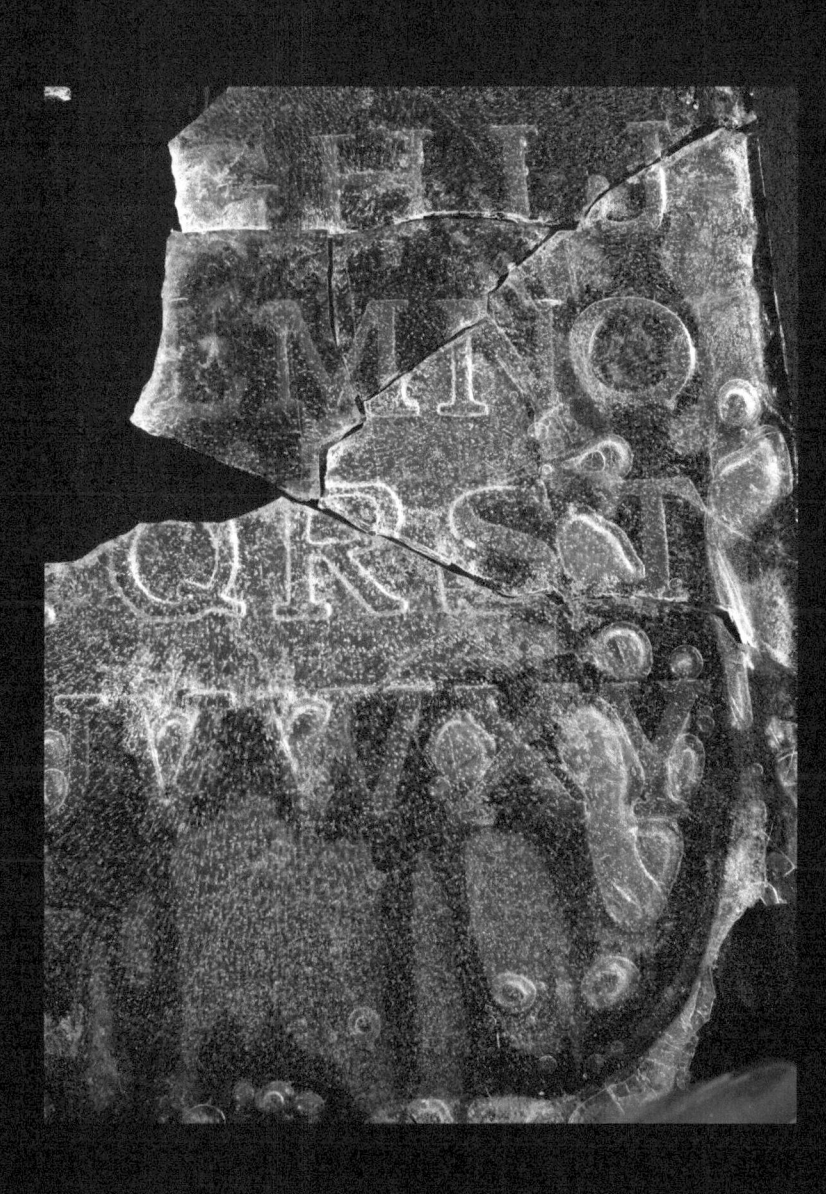

May 6, 2012.

Dappled shadows
cast by the emerging
leaves of a River Birch,
announce the coming of
Spring.

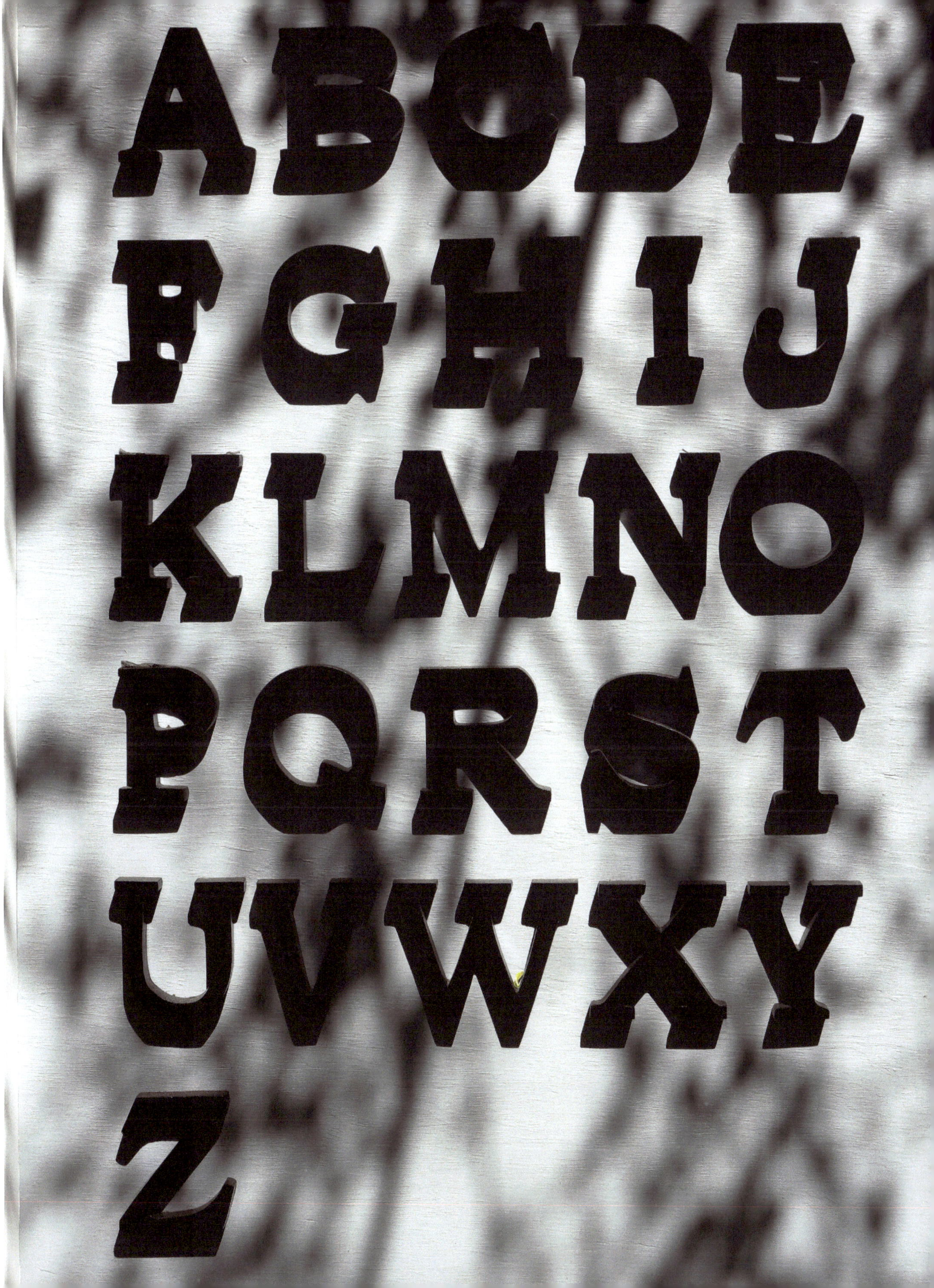

ABCDE

FGHIJ

KLMNO

PQRST

UVWXY

Z

May 11, 2012.

When I first conceived this project I did not imagine that I would photograph anything other than snow falling on the letters. However, as said before, this was an unusually warm winter and the number of snow days were few and far between. I need not have worried. There is always something falling from the sky in upstate New York. In this instance the photograph shows a crop of Maple seed "spinners."

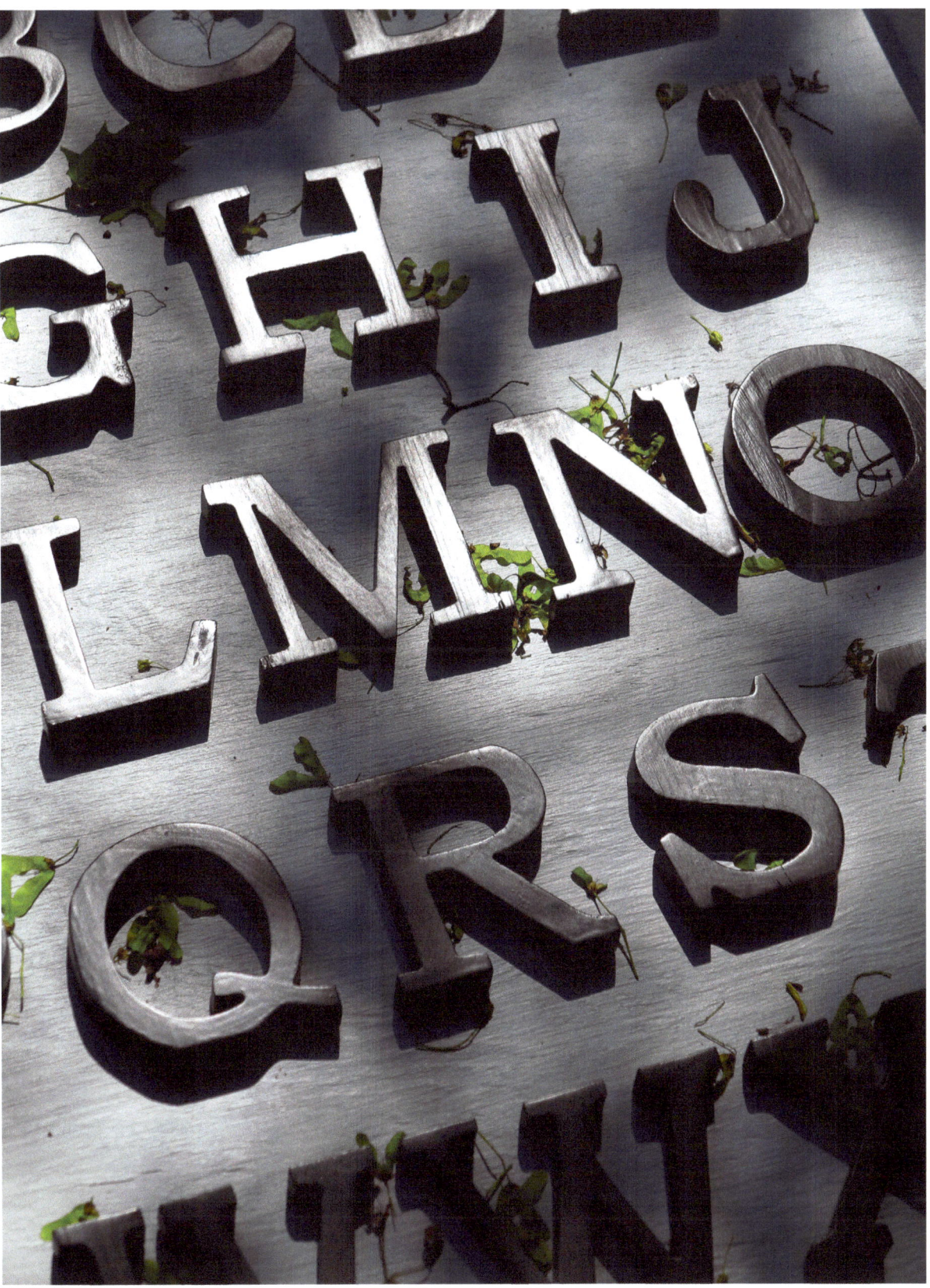

May 25, 2012.

To be followed shortly thereafter by Honey-suckle flowers.

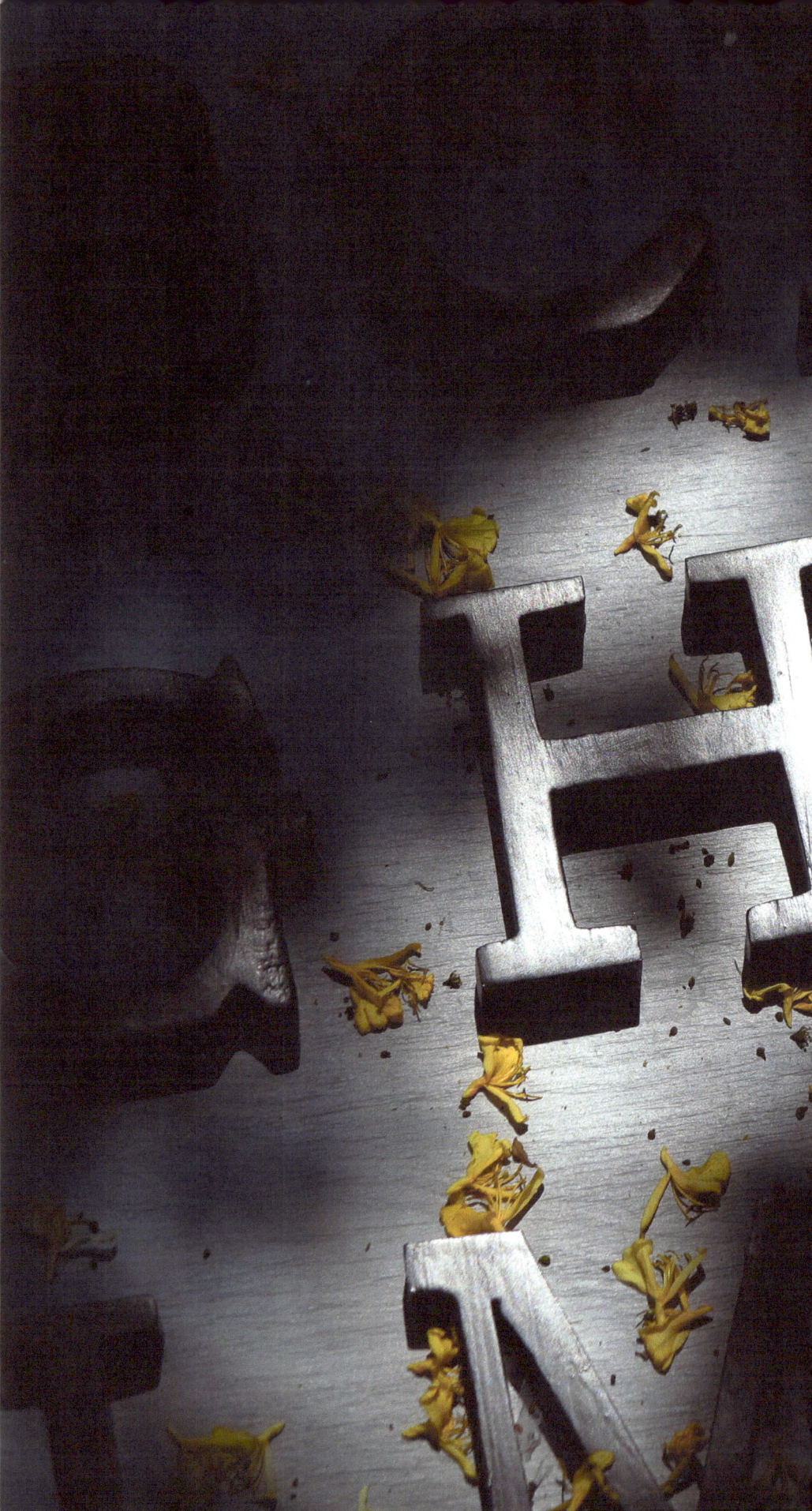

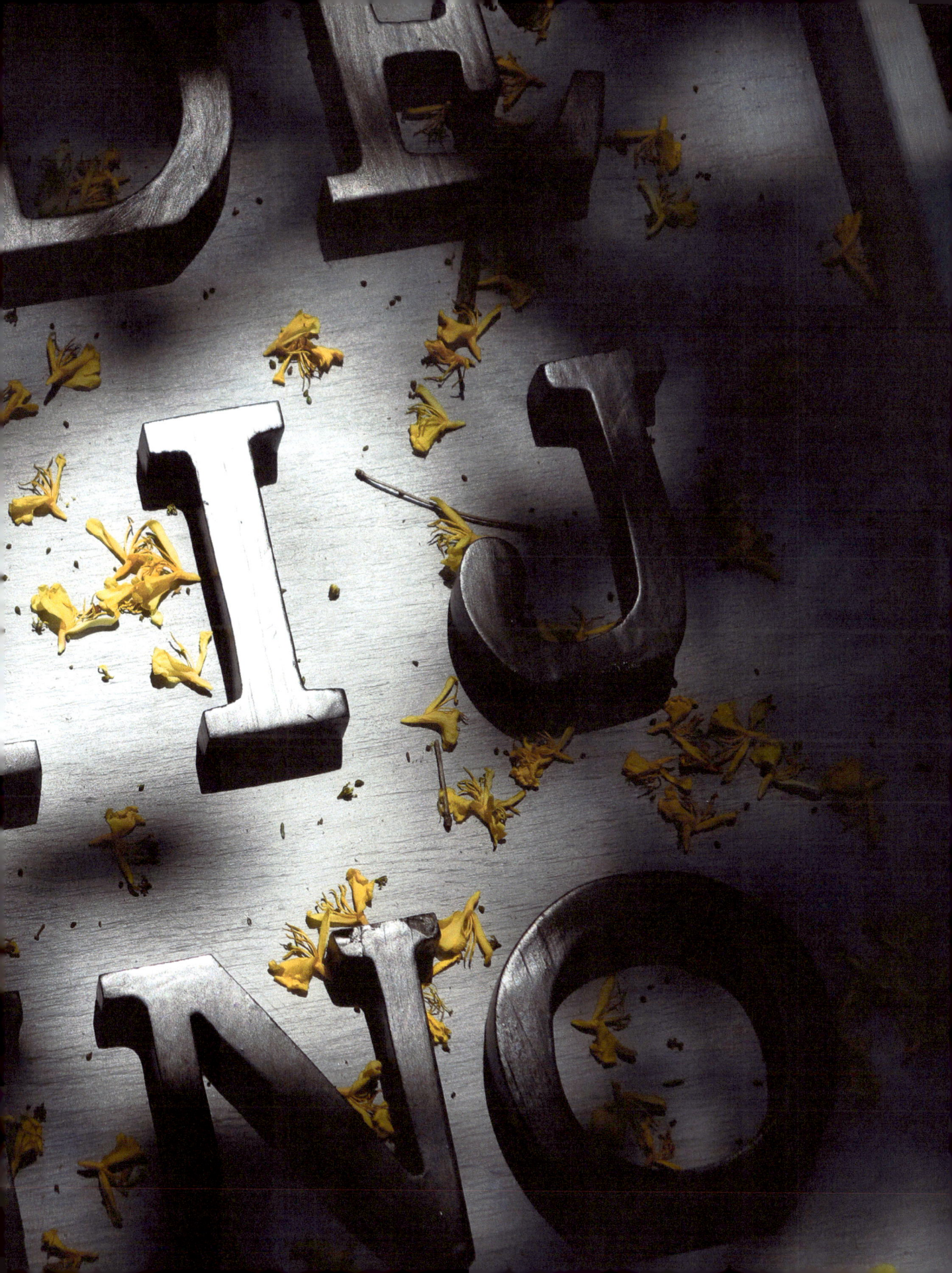

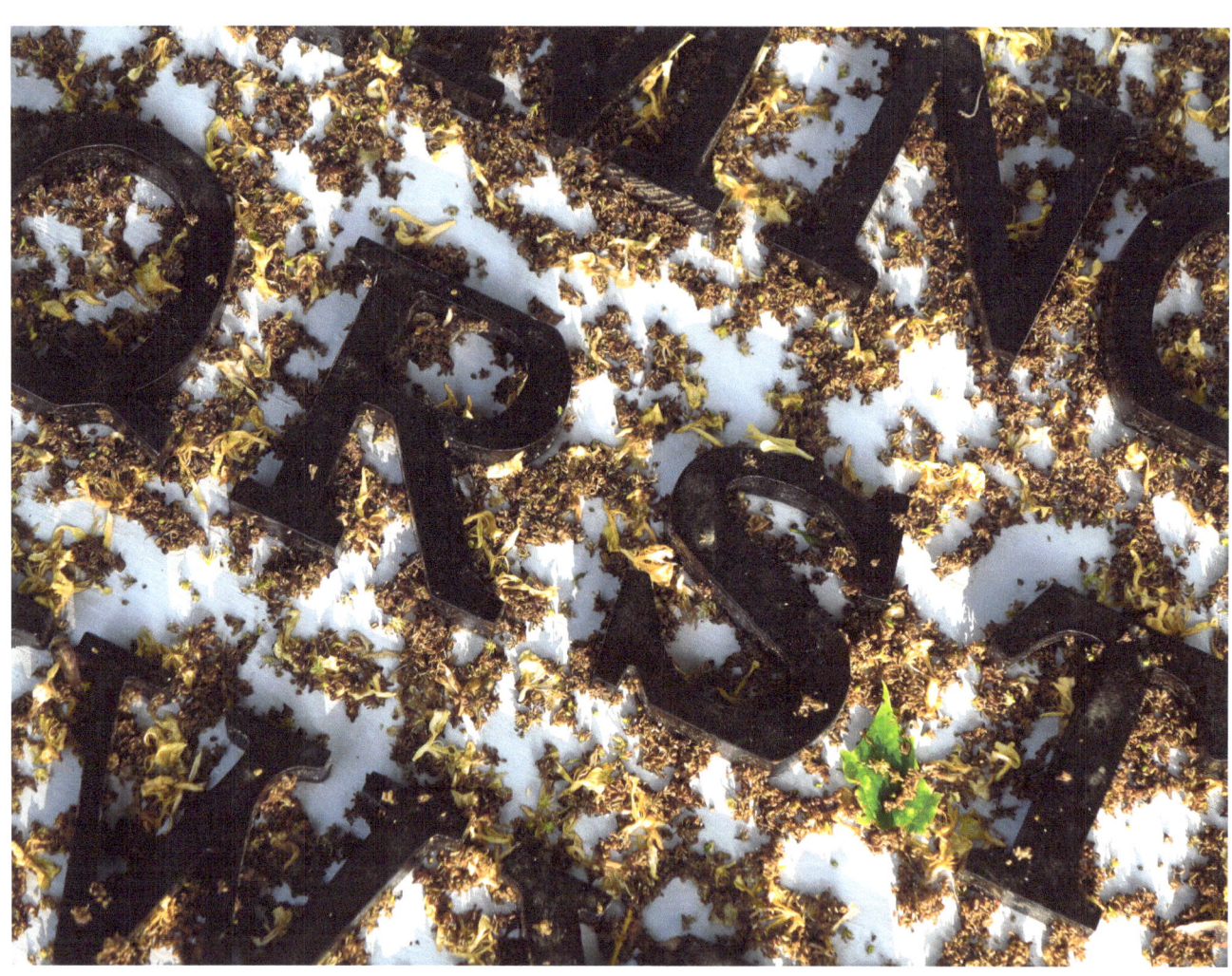

May 28 and 29, 2012.
The Honeysuckle flowers continue their fall now supplemented by seeds.

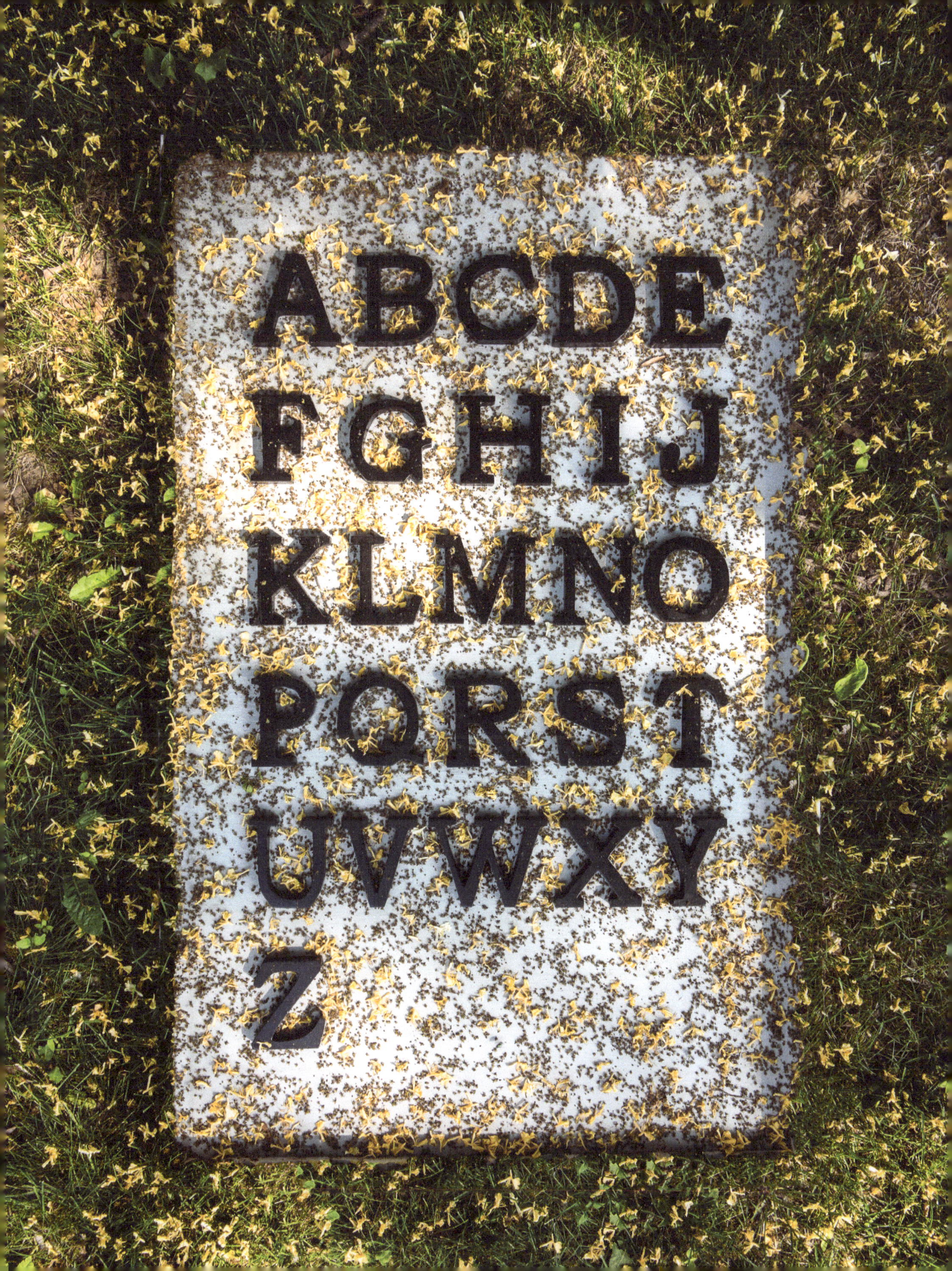
ABCDE
FGHIJ
KLMNO
PQRST
UVWXY
Z

August 6, 2012.

The alphabet goes for a drive! In this case we are visiting the Garden Center in Rochester. The folks there were very kind and permitted me to go scurrying around in their piles of mulch. These images were fun, albeit messy fun, to make. Here we see the alphabet partially buried in a pile of gold mulch.

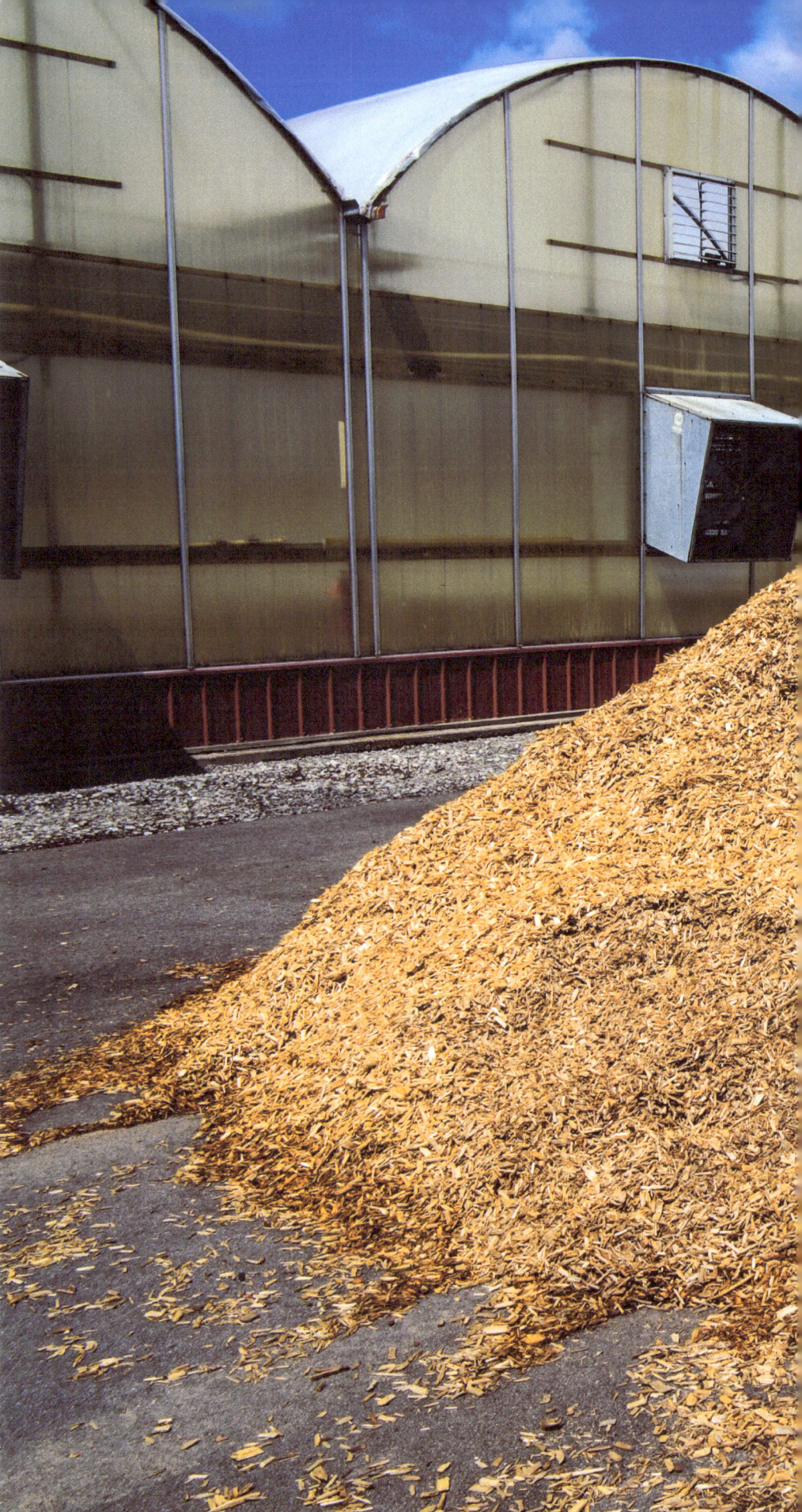

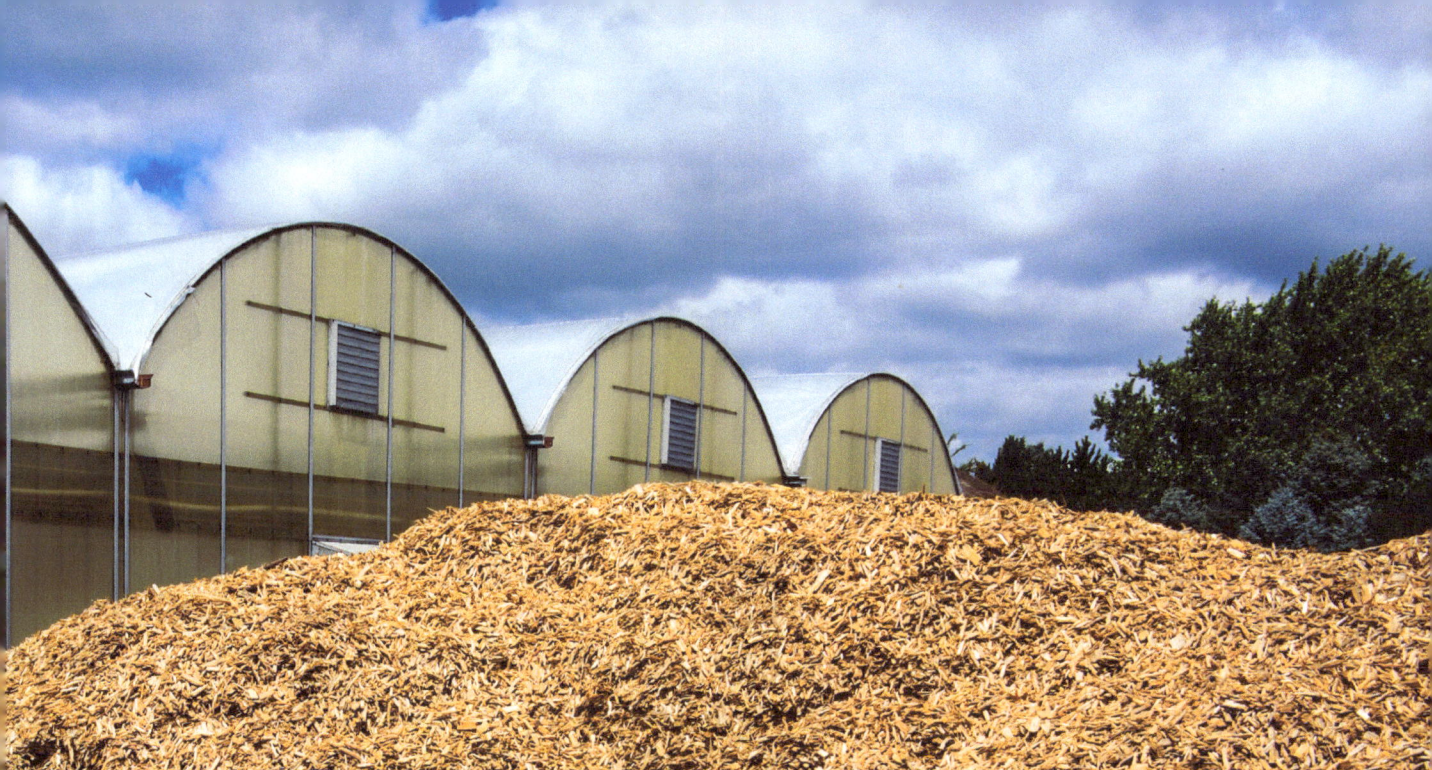

ABCDE
FGHIJ
KLMNO
PQRST
UVWXY
Z

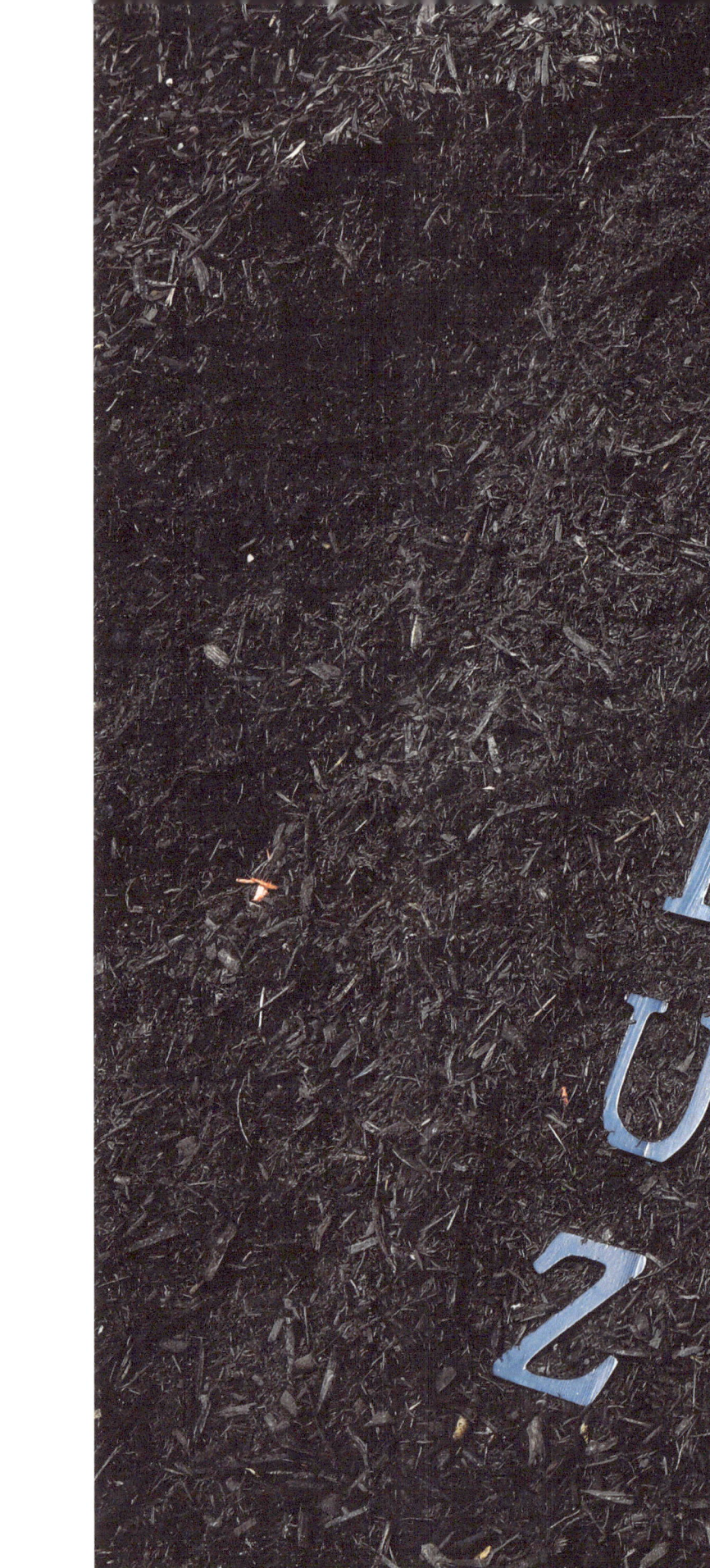

August 6, 2012.
Black mulch.

ABCDE
FGHIJ
KLMNO
QRST
WXY

August 6, 2012.

Back to the gold mulch. The image is rendered in black and white, mimicking the effect of panchromatic film exposed through a blue filter.

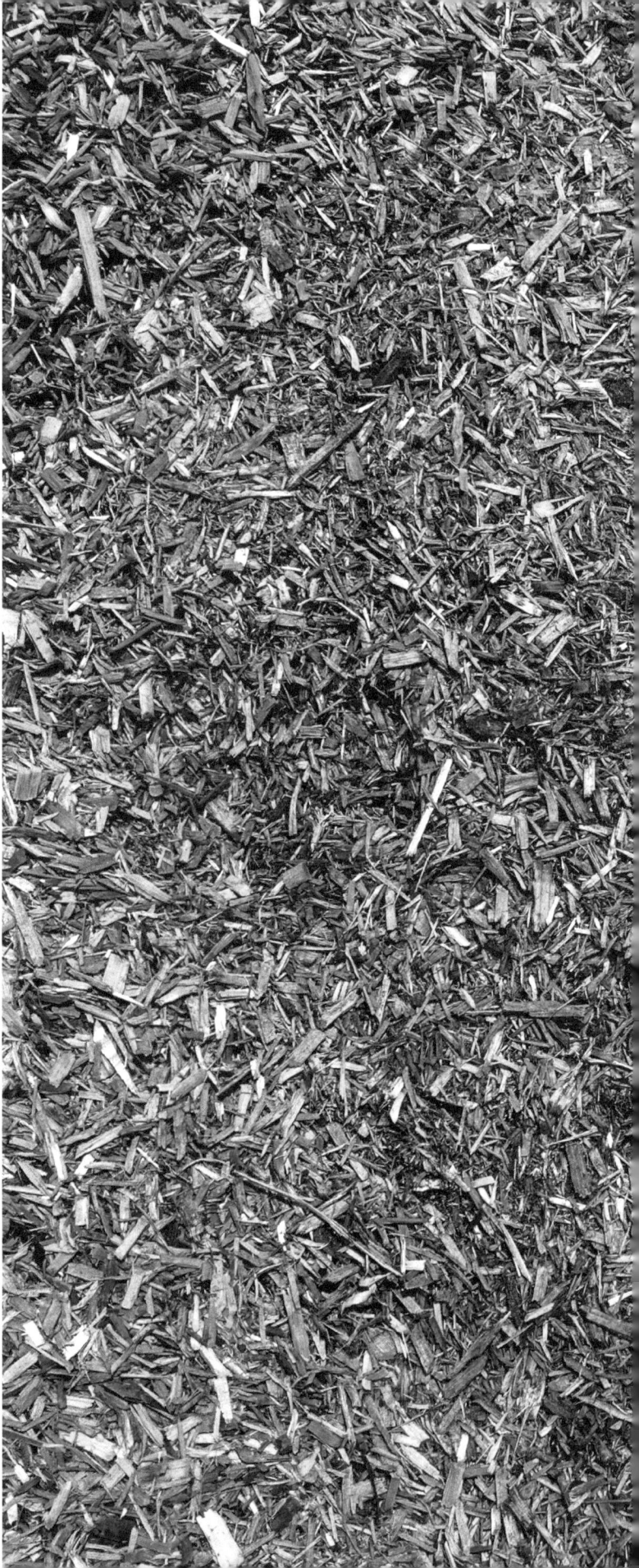

November 1, 2012.

It is now Fall. These beautiful yellow leaves are from the Mulberry tree in the backyard.

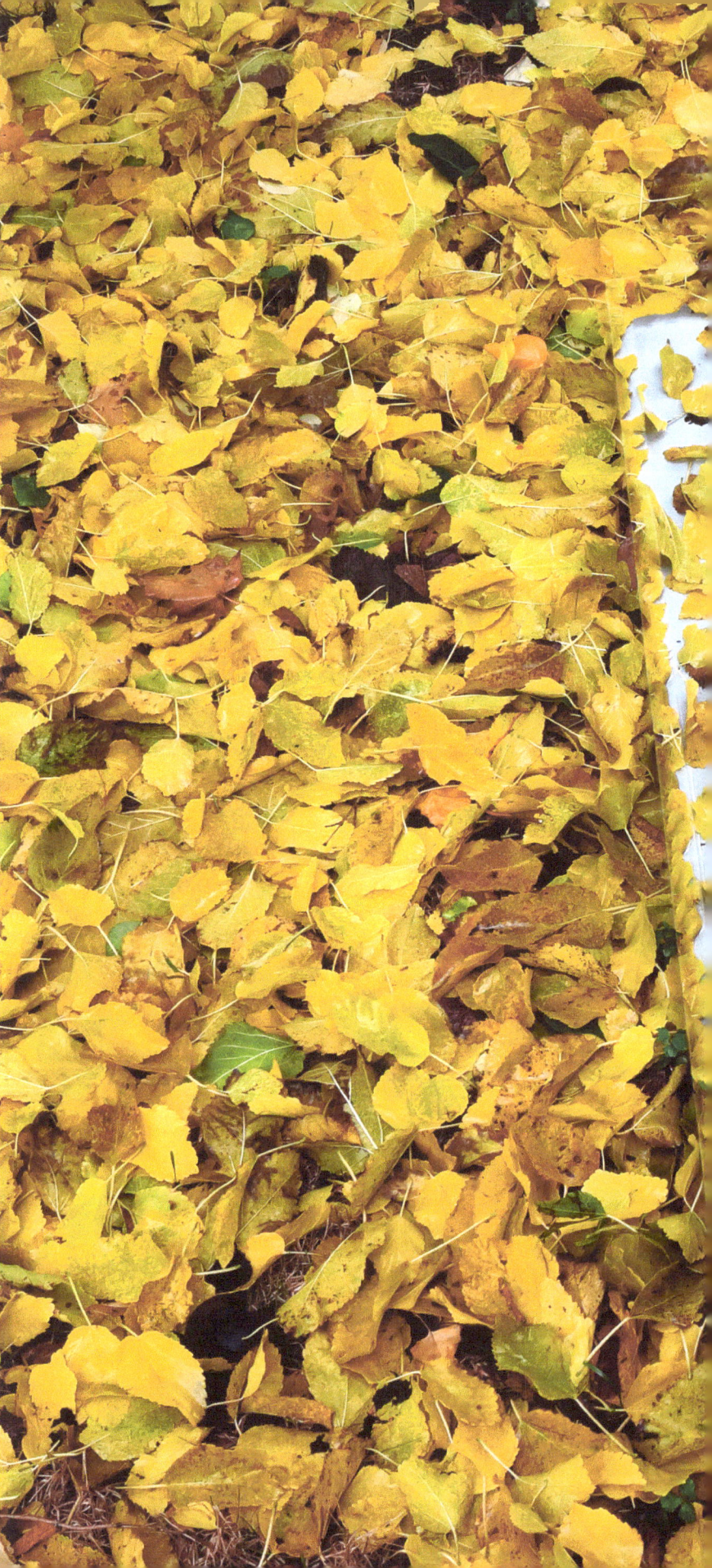

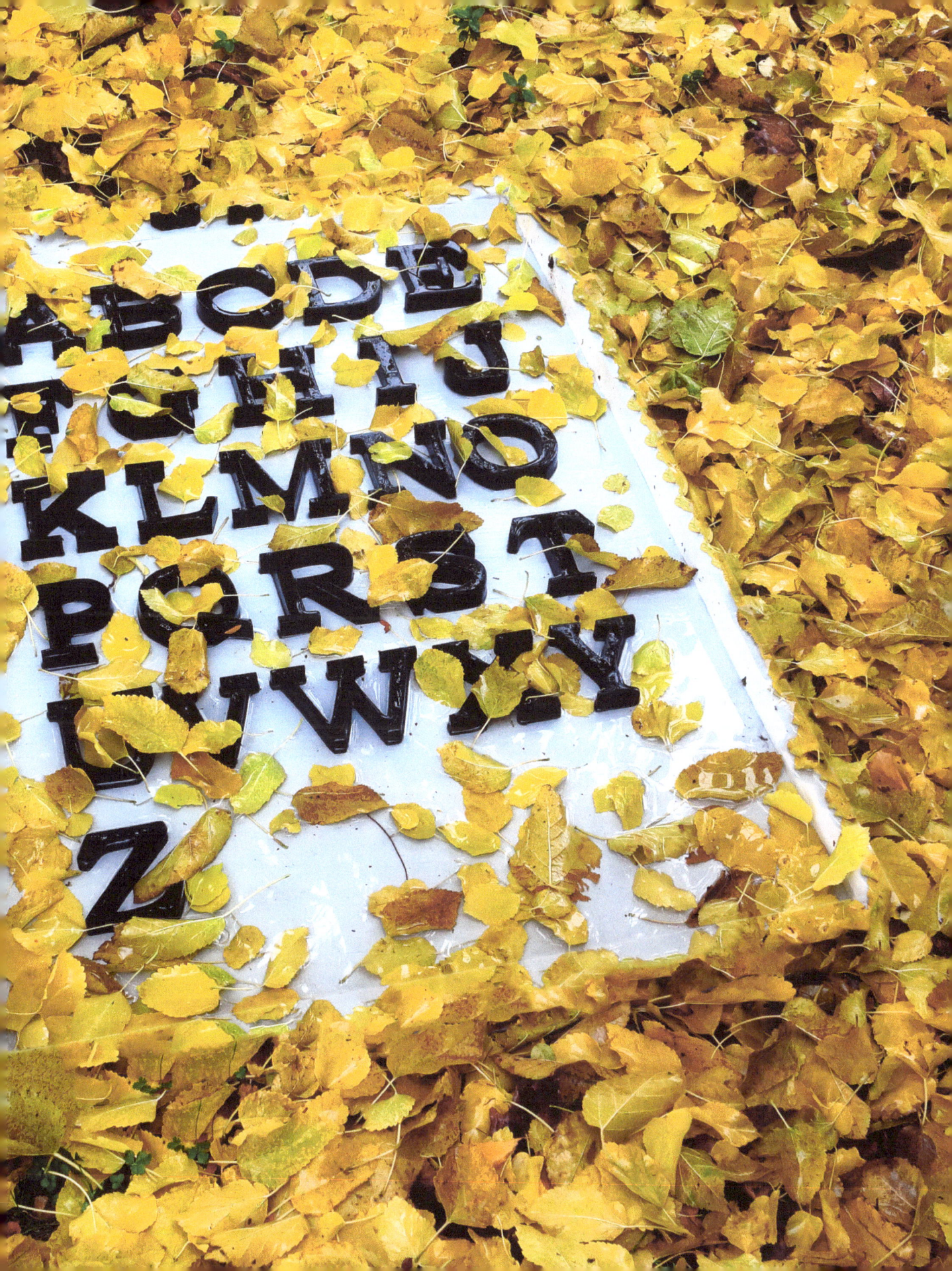

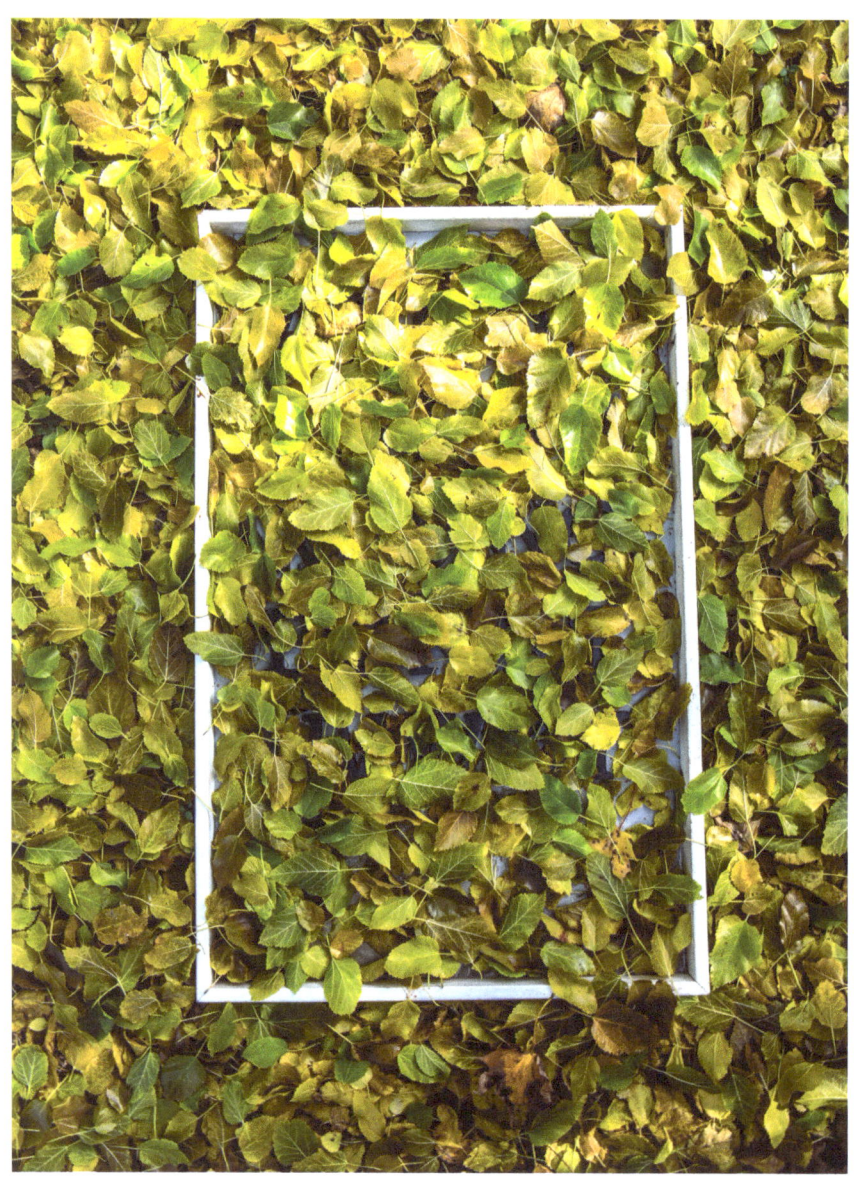

November 7, 2012.
Leaves from the Honeysuckle in the front yard obliterate the letters.

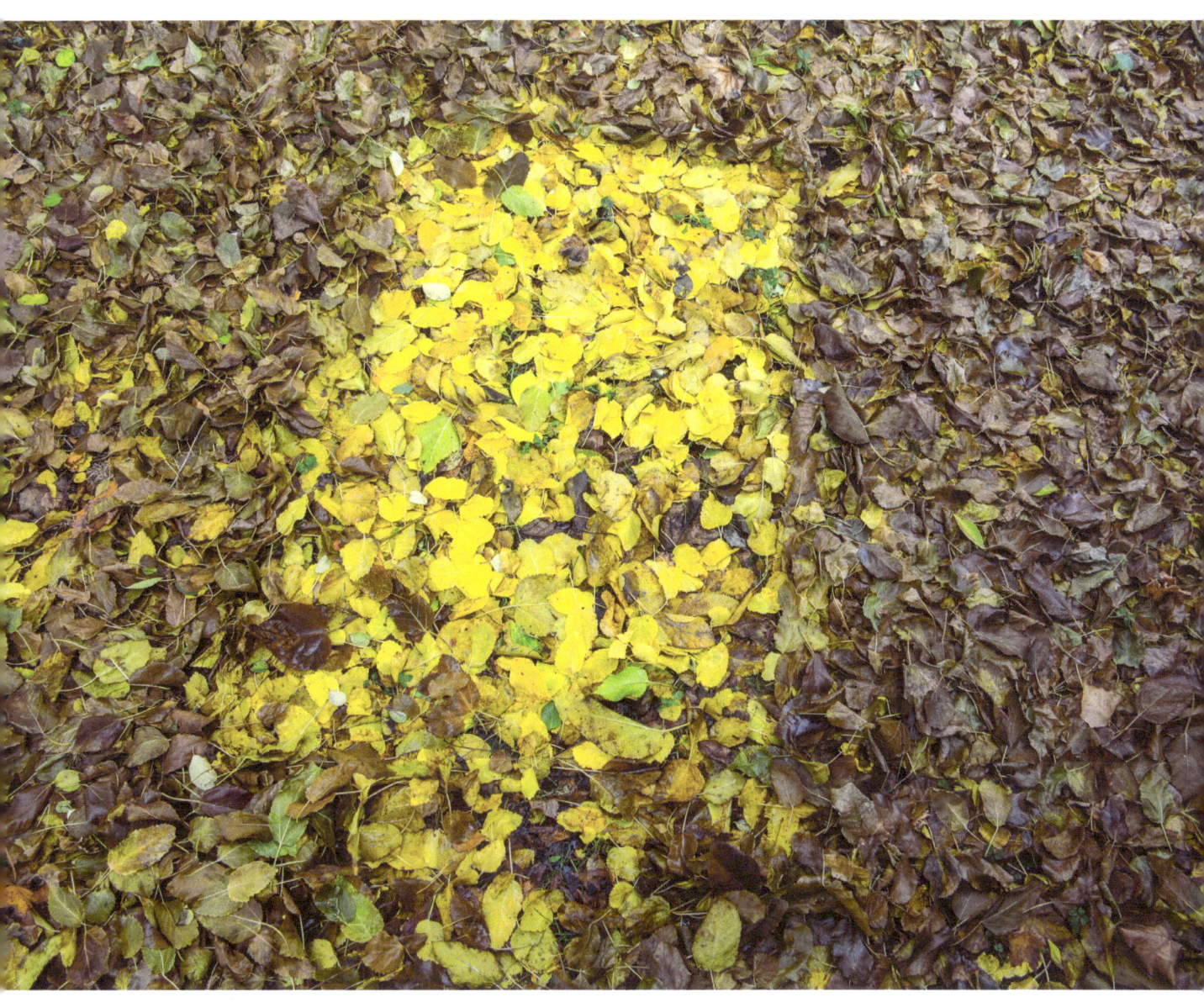

November 11, 2012.
The alphabet was left lying on the lawn for 4 days. When removed, it revealed this trace of its presence.

November 20, 2012.
Time for a good wash.

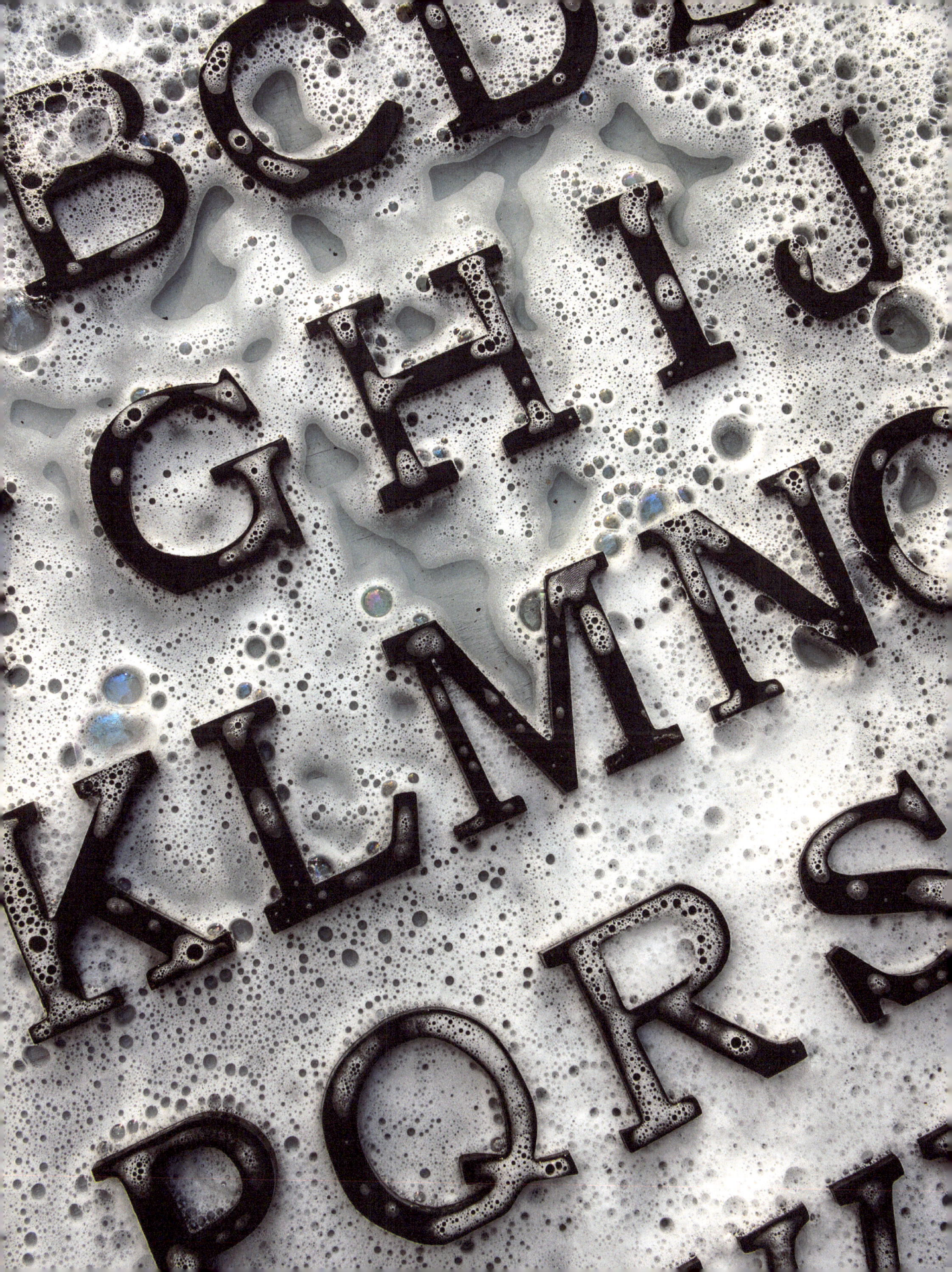

December 22, 2012.

ABCDE
FGHIJ
KLMNO
PQRST
UVWXY
Z

COLOPHON

The typeface employed is Myriad. The book was produced
using Adobe® Creative Suite® 6 software. The images were
processed in Adobe Photoshop® and the book was designed
and prepared for production using Adobe InDesign.® This
print on demand edition of the book is printed in the United
States by Lightning Source. The book is also available in a lim-
ited edition version, printed single-sided on vellum. Contact
clarellen.com for further information. The ongoing *Alphabet*
project is funded in part by Woodland Manufacturing, Inc.